An Authentic American History

PURITANS'

A CATHO〔barcode〕 TIVE

PROGRESS

VOLUME
1

COMPILED BY THE EDITORS
OF ANGELUS PRESS
MATTHEW ANGER
PETER CHOJNOWSKI, PH.D.
REV. FR. KENNETH NOVAK

1492–1770
Europe Crosses the Water

ANGELUS PRESS
2918 TRACY AVENUE, KANSAS CITY, MISSOURI 64109

ANGELUS PRESS

2918 TRACY AVENUE
KANSAS CITY, MISSOURI 64109
PHONE (816) 753-3150
FAX (816) 753-3557
ORDER LINE 1-800-966-7337

ISBN   0-935952-35-7 Series
       0-935952-36-5 Volume 1

FIRST PRINTING—September 1996

Printed in the United States of America

CONTENTS

INTRODUCTION TO THE SERIES

We live in what has been, since 1945 at least, the most important and most powerful nation in the World. Trends, whether political or social, which start in the United States soon spread throughout the globe. But if this is a source of pride to Americans, it is also a great responsibility. For Catholic Americans, the responsibility becomes even greater. In the first case, there is the necessity of ensuring that this great power be a force for good; in the second, there is the added need to spread the Catholic Faith in our native land–thus assisting it throughout the world.

History is the key to understanding men–whether as nations, families, or individuals. Without an employment record, we cannot evaluate a prospective worker; without genealogy, we cannot say much about a given family as it is today. Similarly, without a firm grasp of a nation's history, we cannot understand its present. In the case of America, so many of its present-day policies are based upon factors so deeply buried in our history, that without a good understanding of those factors the present is simply incomprehensible. Yet history (due in part to some of these factors) is probably our most poorly taught subject. Due to other factors, what little of it that is imparted to students is more in the way of a national mythology (with such episodes as Washington and the cherry tree and the Boston Tea Party given more attention than the underlying causes and forces) than serious history–useless for understanding, or for any other purpose than self-praise.

For Catholics, history has an even higher purpose beside. For them, history is the unfolding of God's Will in time, and the attempts of men either to conform themselves to or to resist that Will. As the great Dom Guéranger, author of the monumental *Liturgical Year* points out, "for the Christian there is no purely human history," since "man has been divinely called to the supernatural state. This state is his goal and the chronicles of human kind should therefore exhibit the traces of that supernatural life." Thus the Catholic historian may rely upon the guidance...:

> ...[P]rovided by the Church which always goes before him as a column of light and divinely illuminates all his thoughts. The Christian knows that a close bond unites the Church and the Son of God made man; the Christian knows that the Church has the guarantee of Christ's promise against all errors in her teaching and in the general conduct of Christian society, and that the Holy Spirit animates and leads the Church. It is in her, therefore, that he finds the rule for judging. The true Christian is not surprised by the weakness of churchmen or by their temporal abuses, because he knows that God has decided to tolerate the weeds in His field until the harvest....But he knows where the direction, the spirit, and the divine instinct of the Church are manifested. He receives them, he accepts them, he professes them bravely and applies them in his narration of history. Therefore, he never betrays them, he never sacrifices them, he considers good what the Church judges as good and bad what the Church judges as bad. He does not care about the sarcasm or clamor of shortsighted cowards. Other historians will stubbornly observe only the political side

of events, and so will descend to the pagan point of view. But the Christian historian will remain firm, because he has the initial certainty that he is not mistaken. [He knows that] Christ is at home in history; [that is why] he must not fear condemning the thousands of calumnies which have made history a huge conspiracy against truth....It is necessary to be prepared to fight; if one is not brave enough to do that, then that person should refrain from writing history (Guéranger, *The Christian Sense of History*, pp.17-18, 53-54).

The good Benedictine gives us a second important premise:

The supreme disgrace of the Christian historian would be to take the ideas of his time as criteria for evaluation and to apply them to judging the past. [In this way non-Christians] succeed in dragging Catholics into their systems, and are jubilant because of the progress they have made in imposing their language and their ideas (*ibid.*, 36 and 59).

Adherence to these principles has produced such great historians as Hilaire Belloc, Bernard Faÿ, William Thomas Walsh, and Christopher Hollis, to say nothing of the great Dom Guéranger himself. But American Catholic historians have generally refrained from exploring their own national history with these principles, preferring instead to adopt the analysis of their non-Catholic colleagues, save when looking at purely Catholic topics (and sometimes not then).

It is the belief of the editors that the facts of US history show how Catholic government, whether English, French, or Spanish, was gradually crowded out on this continent watered by the blood of Catholic martyrs from all parts of Europe who first planted the cross of Christ here. A candid examination of the facts of US history will bear our contention out. For America is not as yet really a nation. It is in fact a religion–Americanism, described thusly by Dr. John Rao:

> "Americanism" is a religion which both major elements of the American "soul"–secularized Puritanism and Anglo-Saxon conservatism–have helped to develop. "Americanism" is a religion that adores the United States as the incarnation of the secularized Puritan vision of paradise. It is a religion that simultaneously adores the bland, materialistic, catch-all unity that stems from the Anglo-Saxon drive for stability and integration. "Americanism" is an evangelical religion that wishes the rest of the world to be converted to its doctrines (*Americanism*, p.3).

As a revealed religion Catholicism must claim a monopoly of truth; she cannot be tolerant of error, of false religions. Americanism, being a rival Faith, must inevitably be an opponent of Catholicism. As Dr. Rao further opines:

> [It] is, and always has been, a danger to the Church of Rome. Indeed, the threat that it poses to Catholicism may be the most pressing experienced in the past few centuries of revolution (*loc. cit.*).

Having said all of this, it must be pointed out that opposition to the religion of Americanism is not the same thing as disloyalty to the country. If anything, pursuit of the Americanist religious ideals has involved this country in innumerable foreign and domestic disputes, any one of which could easily have destroyed us. Moreover, for a Catholic resident in a non-Catholic country, a desire to convert his nation from its error constitutes real patriotism, just as a convert's desire to see his parents accept the truth of the Faith is the cornerstone of his love for them.

It is vital, then, for Catholics, especially young Catholics, to have a good and proper understanding of their country's history. To exercise their patriotism, they must work for the conversion of the US; to do this effectively, they must understand the forces and events which brought forth not only the religion of Americanism and the country itself, but also the sort of Catholicism which, in 300 years, failed so dismally to bring this conversion about.

One of the most exciting and positive notes of our history, however, is that the American continents have provided a place wherein native and European, African, and Asian cultures have mingled, and from which a vital spirit emerged. In those areas evangelized properly, the results have been extraordinary. Two models have been offered for this mingling: the Catholic, wherein the constituent elements retain their integrity while enriching one another, and the Americanist, wherein the ultimate result is intended to create a conformity based upon the lowest common denominator: money.

In this series of books, it is hoped that a beginning will be made toward a Catholic view of American history. Obviously, such a vast topic cannot be adequately explored in the little space available to us. But what can be done (and what the editors hopes to have accomplished) is to reinterpret the better known episodes of our history in accordance with the Faith, and to point up lesser-known details which will give factual proof of the truth of this reinterpretation.

Unfortunately, so poor has so much of the standard historical education been in recent decades, that many names, places and dates which were common knowledge not long ago will have been forgotten. Hence, for best results, this series should be used alongside a standard encyclopedia. The names and places in italics can then be looked up for further knowledge.

The editors do not pretend to have written the final word in this matter; it is no small task to reverse five centuries of misinterpretation and outright lies. But if this present work will inspire other, abler hands to lend their pens to this work, they will have succeeded.

At any rate, it will be helpful, before we begin our survey, to look at the continents of Europe, America, and Africa on the eve of the great discovery which would bring them all together.

EUROPE

The Europe of 1492 was a continent in the midst of change. In the West, Catholicism reigned supreme from Iceland to Russia. In many ways, the ideals of medieval Christendom, although shaken by the Great Schism (with its scandal of three popes at once) and the Renaissance (with its rediscovery of pagan literature and morality), remained. The Middle Ages were suffused with Catholicism in a way which the world has never seen—before or since. This does not mean that they were perfect, or that men were any less sinners than they are now. What it does mean is that they were clearer as to their goals than were either their ancestors or their descendants. As Kenelm Digby observes in *Mores Catholici*, "...the avowed object of all government in ages of faith was to secure glory to God, and peace on earth to men of goodwill." The Catholic religion admitted of no other.

The kings themselves, hereditary for the most part, were not merely the equivalents of our heads of state. For just as papal and imperial authority were considered to be divine in origin, so too was royal. Yet the kings often had little power: no power of income tax, nor of regulation, nor of the secret police, nor of so many of the myriad interferences we have come to accept as the rightful appurtenances of governmental power. Instead, as Kenelm Digby (*op. cit.* p.99) says:

...the whole state was founded on the pacific type of the best kingdom. The pacific character of royal majesty was a religious idea, emanating from what was believed of the celestial dominations and powers; for it was a devotional exercise in reparation of the sins of anger, passion, and revenge, to offer to God the peace, mildness and tranquillity of the thrones. The Christian religion had put everything in its place, so that the hierarchy of men was as complete as that of angels in the order shown by Dionysius. As in the latter, thrones are after Seraphim and Cherubim, so in the state, physical force was regarded after love and science. In the ancient Christian sculpture, dominations, which command angels, and principalities, which rule over men, are represented with crowns and scepters; but powers which command the Satanic race are shown with spear and shield, since the devil only yields to force. Therefore, the crown and scepter were the symbols of royal power, and the maxim was "'Tis more kingly to obtain peace than to enforce conditions by constraint."

For this reason, the king had three roles: in a sense, he had a demi-priestly character, conferred by his coronation. He was firstly the defender of the Church within his realm. A sort of sub-diaconal character was his, and various kings were often traditionally canons of one or several of their cathedral cities. Kings also often had liturgical roles, such as foot-washing on Maundy Thursday, an honored place in Corpus Christi and other processions, and special Mass prayers said for them. In a few cases, he was believed to have miraculous powers. So the Kings of England and France cured scrofula (called "The King's Evil"), the King of Denmark cured epilepsy, the King of Hungary, jaundice, and the Holy Roman Emperor, successor of Charlemagne, was said to have some control over the weather (so in Germany fine warm weather is called *Kaiserswetter*). Isabel of Spain's ancestors, the Kings of Castile, were resorted to by the possessed for exorcism, as we see in Alvarez Pelayo's 1340 work, *Speculum regum*, written to King Alphonso XI:

> It is said that the kings of France and of England possess a [healing] power; likewise the most pious kings of Spain, from whom you are descended, possess a power which acts on the demoniacs and certain sick persons suffering from divers ills. When a small child, I myself saw your grandfather king Sancho [Sancho II, 1284-1295], who brought me up, place his foot upon the throat of a demoniac who proceeded to heap insults upon him; and then, by reading words taken from a little book, drive out the demon from this woman, and leave her perfectly healed. (Quoted in Marc Bloch, *The Royal Touch*, p.88).

His Majesty's second role was as supreme judge. The Court of Queen's Bench is a relic of this in Commonwealth countries–indeed, our very word "court" hearkens back to the king sitting in judgment over cases, with all his chief men around him. Yet he could not be arbitrary: each of his provinces must be ruled in accordance with their own laws– or Roman law if that was accepted there. Law was considered to be something immutable, which could be discovered, but never created. So true was this that the Assizes of Jerusalem, the legal code of the Latin Kingdom of that city, were declared to be a recovery of previous law, rather than a new creation for a new kingdom. Nor was the king above the law: such things as *Magna Carta* and various Golden Bulls were not considered as new limitations of the king's power, but rather a return to previously existing balance. Since the king had little power at his command, he must either hear cases in his own residence, send out judges to the different provinces of his realm, or else invest various local notables with judicial power. Lack of a real standing army

2015

generally reduced his ability to discipline offending nobles to merely declaring such "outlaws" who might be preyed upon by any other noble strong enough to do so.

This last brings us to the king's third role: warlord. He was chief of whatever soldiery he happened to have on hand: if he wished to go to war with a neighboring nation or to go on Crusade, he must summon his chief nobles with their retainers, or else hire mercenaries. Both of these were often dangerous propositions. Thus it is that until the Hundred Years' War, we see little in the way of major wars between Christian kings, although there was plenty of local warfare between barons.

The king's role, then, was that of orchestra conductor. A good king, like St. Louis, was able to benefit his subjects greatly through force of personality; a bad one was unable, generally, to do more than make the lives of his courtiers unpleasant. Would that the same might be said of chief executives today! The kings gathered around themselves courts. These consisted of the ruler's friends, servants, and the great men of his realm. One thinks immediately of King Arthur's Round Table, the Paladins of Charlemagne, and the warriors clustered around Hrothgar in *Beowulf*, but the much attenuated descendants of such groups may be found today in institutions like the British Privy Council and the Danish Council of State. Within these amorphous bands, the king carried out his main functions: observing the rites of the Church, ruling on judicial cases brought to him, and occasionally deciding on military action.

As time progressed, these particular functions became more specialized, and eventually developed into quasi-departments or ministries of state. From this simple beginning have derived the great central administrations with which we are familiar; in time, these would do away with the kings. Today, only the largely ceremonial British royal household,

and the pragmatic Roman Curia survive in anything like
their original form.

It is important to remember that just as Christendom
was one body in religious matters, so it was in temporal
matters also. This is admirably summed up by James, Vis-
count Bryce, in his *The Holy Roman Empire* (pp.102-105):

> The realistic philosophy, and the needs of a time when
> the only notion of civil or religious order was submission
> to authority, required the World State to be a monarchy:
> tradition, as well as the continued existence of a part of
> the ancient institutions, gave the monarch the name of
> Roman Emperor. A king could not be universal sover-
> eign, for there were many kings: the Emperor must be
> universal, for there had never been but one Emperor; he
> had in older and brighter days been the actual lord of the
> civilized world; the seat of his power was placed beside
> that of the spiritual autocrat of Christendom. His func-
> tions will be seen most clearly if we deduce them from
> the leading principle of medieval mythology [as the ig-
> norant call it], the exact correspondence of earth and
> heaven. As God, in the midst of the celestial hierarchy,
> rules blessed spirits in Paradise, so the Pope, His vicar,
> raised above priests, bishops, metropolitans, reigns over
> the souls of mortal men below. But as God is Lord of
> earth as well as of heaven, so must he (the *Imperator
> coelestis*) be represented by a second earthly viceroy, the
> Emperor (*Imperator terrenus*), whose authority shall be
> of and for this present life. And as in this present world
> the soul cannot act save through the body, while yet the
> body is no more than an instrument and means for the
> soul's manifestation, so there must be a rule and care of
> men's bodies as well as of their souls, yet subordinated
> always to the well-being of that element which is the
> purer and more enduring. It is under the emblem of soul
> and body that the relation of the papal and imperial power
> is presented to us throughout the Middle Ages. The Pope,

as God's vicar in matters spiritual, is to lead men to eternal life; the Emperor, as vicar in matters temporal, must so control them in their dealings with one another that they are able to pursue undisturbed the spiritual life, and thereby attain the same supreme and common end of everlasting happiness. In view of this object his chief duty is to maintain peace in the world, while towards the Church his position is that of Advocate or Patron, a title borrowed from the practice adopted by churches and monasteries of choosing some powerful baron to protect their lands and lead their tenants in war. The functions of Advocacy are twofold: at home to make the Christian people obedient to the priesthood, and to execute priestly decrees upon heretics and sinners; abroad to propagate the faith among the heathen, not sparing to use carnal weapons. Thus does the Emperor answer in every point to his antitype the Pope, his power being yet of a lower rank, created on the analogy of the papal....Thus the Holy Roman Church and the Holy Roman Empire are one and the same thing, seen from different sides; and Catholicism, the principle of the universal Christian society, is also Romanism...

This has specific reference to our own continent. Gary Potter defines it admirably in modern terms (*In Reaction*, p.55):

Words express ideas, and some of them now being quoted signify notions likely to be totally foreign to anyone unfamiliar with history prior to a few decades ago: "world emperor," "imperial office."....This is not the place to lay out all the history needed to be known for thoroughly grasping the notions. However, the principal one was adumbrated by Our Lord Himself in the last command His followers received from Him: to make disciples of *all* the nations. In a word, the idea of a universal Christian commonwealth is what we are talking about.

To date it has never existed. Today there is not even a Christian government anywhere. However, from the conversion of Constantine until August, 1806–with an interruption (in the West) from Romulus Augustulus in 476 to Charlemagne in 800–there was *the* Empire. It was the heart of what was once known as Christendom. Under its aegis serious European settlement of the Western Hemisphere began, and the Americas' native inhabitants were first baptized, which is why the feathered cloak of Montezuma is in a museum in Vienna.

The first time Christendom had set out to colonize a territory outside of Western Europe was during the course of the First Crusade in 1099. At that time, while the modern nationalities of Europe were in existence, they were seen by their members as being at least theoretically subordinate to their common obedience to the Holy Empire, the *Res Publica Christiana*. Although various of the armies of the First Crusade were lead by Lorrainers, French, English Normans, and Italian Normans, and in later days German, French, and English rulers would lead swarms of multi-national crusaders to the Holy Land, there was never any question of annexing the new lands to one of the constituent kingdoms of the Empire. Instead, the lands freed from the Turk were organized into independent Crusader states: the Kingdom of Jerusalem, and its vassal counties of Edessa, Tripoli, and Antioch.

Being the common property of Christendom, the Kingdom of Jerusalem was organized as the prototypical feudal state. For all that the king was crowned in the Basilica of the Nativity in Bethlehem, his powers were limited. His three chief officers, the Seneschal, Marshal, and Constable, each wielded considerable power. The lords of the constituent fiefs, gathered together in the High Court, were a strong check on the king's will, as was the Court of the Burgesses, to which belonged citizens of the different towns. The Patriarch of Jerusalem and the Grand Masters of the three Military Orders (Knights Templar, Knights Hospitaller, and Teutonic Knights) were similarly placed. All in all, the historian must agree with Donald Attwater's description of the Kingdom's administration as "a good example...wise, just, and moderate."

But this first attempt at colonization would fail. Internal disunion could perhaps have been remedied. But the growing national disunity of the states of Christendom, whose joint effort was essential to the Kingdom's survival, doomed it. By 1291, the last cities held by the Crusaders had fallen. With the exception of the 1918-1948 British Mandate, the Holy Land has been out of Christian hands ever since.

This disunity continued; it led to the fratricidal Hundred Years' War between England and France, the War of the Roses in the former country, ongoing strife between Guelphs (Papal supporters) and Ghibellines (Imperial supporters) in Germany and Italy, and at last the Great Schism in the very Papacy itself. The same friction between emerging, centralizing nations led directly to the fall of Constantinople to the Turks in 1453, and permitted them to occupy all Europe south of the Danube River.

But by 1492, a great deal of this had been papered over; Alexander VI, the much maligned Borgia Pope, was on the throne of Peter; Frederick III, last of the Emperors to be crowned at Rome, was reigning in Vienna. Charles VIII of France had married Anne of Brittany, uniting her land—the last major independent fief—to the French throne. In England, Henry VII, first of the Tudors, was imposing unity on the country after defeating and killing the rightful King, Richard III, in 1485. While all these men were attempting to consolidate their respective realms by centralizing power under the royal administrations we have just discussed,

Ferdinand and Isabel of Spain, having united Aragon and Castile by their marriage, were ending the age-old struggle against the Moors. The year of 1492 saw the fall of the last Moorish stronghold, Granada, to the Spanish. The Canary, Azores, and Madeira Islands had already been discovered and partially colonized by this year. An Italian mariner, Christopher Columbus, wished to go further in that direction, and blaze new trade routes to the Far East; these would replace the ones occupied by the Turks, and allow the Faith to expand in heretofore unknown areas. Freed of the Moorish problem, Ferdinand and Isabel were disposed to back him.

The Portuguese, during the course of the 1400's, had themselves been busy exploring. Under the patronage of the King's brother, *Prince Henry the Navigator* (1394-1460), the Azores, Madeiras, and Cape Verdes were discovered as mentioned. Portuguese sailors continued to journey south along the African coast, until in 1486, *Bartholomew Diaz* discovered the Cape of Good Hope. The East lay waiting. But it should be noted that Prince Henry was not interested only in trade with the Far East. As Grand Master of the Order of Christ (the Portuguese branch of the Templars which survived when that order was suppressed), he committed his ships and sailors to finding out the strength of Islam in the regions they explored, to attempt to contact Christian allies (if any were present) and to spread the Faith among the heathen. So it was that his caravels bore the red Crusader's cross, as their voyages of discovery were considered continuations of that conflict.

THE AMERICAS

Due to the lack of written records, a veil is drawn across the face of pre-Columbian America. Although the commonly held belief among academics is that there was little or no contact between the Americas and the rest of the world, some scholars do maintain otherwise. The history of the Americas is quite as and even more interesting from this point of view. In the article "Mexico," in the *Catholic Encyclopedia*, (X, p.252), there is a fascinating account of pre-Columbian Mexican religion. Some of their traditions closely parallel various stories from Genesis, and represent their particular remnants of the original revelation given the first men. But other elements have a later origin:

> In the history of the nations of ancient Mexico the coming of Quetzalcoatl marks a distinct era. He was said to have come from the province of Panuco, a white man, of great stature, broad brow, large eyes, long black hair, rounded beard, and dressed in a tunic covered with black and red crosses. Chaste, intelligent, a lover of peace, versed in the arts and sciences, he preached by his example and doctrine a new religion which inculcated fasting and penance, love and reverence for the Divinity, practice of virtue, and hatred of vice.

He went on to predict the coming of white men at a particular time and place (which "just happened" to be those where came Cortez) who would overthrow their old gods. He was driven out, and went to Yucatan with the same message; among the Mayans he was called Kukulcan. From his time in both areas dates the native veneration of the Cross, and in various places there were practiced rites he had introduced, suggestive of our baptism, confession, and communion. The Mayans who practiced the latter called the bread *Toyolliatlacual*: "food of our souls." The author of the article supposes that Quetzalcoatl was a 10th or 11th century Norse priest, driven off course perhaps from the Northern voyages. Others suggest that he was some disciple of the Irish St. Brendan the Navigator, or even the Saint himself. Whatever

the case, the implications of the song written by Cauch, High
Priest of Tixcayon long before the Spanish came are clear:

> There shall come the sign of a god who dwells on high,
> And the cross which illumined the world shall be made
> manifest;
> The worship of false gods shall cease.
> Your father comes, O Itzalanos!
> Your brother comes, O Itzalanos!
> Receive your bearded guests from the East,
> Who come to bring the sign of God.
> God it is who comes to us, meek and holy.

It is interesting to note that Our Lady appeared at Guadalupe in the traditional garb of an Aztec princess. This 1531
apparition was the signal for mass conversion. Ancient Peru
also had a Quetzalcoatl-like figure, Viracocha, who was said
to have been an old bearded white man wearing a robe and
carrying a staff.

The Vikings, while still pagan, had chased Irish monks
from Iceland. Upon their settlement of Greenland, they found
evidence that the same group had preceded them, and then
fled westward. According to the *Vinland Saga*, the Indians
the Norse later encountered on the coast of North America
informed them of white bearded men in the interior, who
wearing robes carried crosses in procession. The Vikings assumed that these were still more of the same. They themselves maintained a diocese in Greenland from the tenth century until the 1400's, when the Greenland colony died out.
We have, of course, no way of knowing what, if any, missionary activity they undertook, whether collectively or via
lone individuals.

Then there is the famous tale of Madoc ap Owain
Gwynedd, the legendary Welsh prince who many claim led
a party of colonists to North America in 1170. The legends
of "white Indians" bearing tattered Missals, crucifixes, rosa-

ries, etc., appear to have some basis in fact: Roman coins (then in circulation in Wales) have been discovered in Kentucky, where such a group was rumored to exist around Louisville in the 18th century. Lewis and Clark were very surprised by the Caucasian appearance of many of the Mandan Indians; artist George Catlin, who lived among them before their near destruction by smallpox and knew them better than any other white man, claimed their language contained a great many Welsh words. Whatever the case, the Daughters of the American Revolution felt the story had enough proof to erect a monument to Madoc at the supposed site of his landing in Mobile Bay.

There are further supposed traces of Japanese, Chinese, African, and even Phoenician visits to the American coasts before Columbus. But regardless of whether or not such voyagers arrived, it was Columbus who started the movement which would make America an integral part of the civilization of Europe.

There were, however, civilizations in the Americas already: the bloody theocracy of the Aztecs, and the ant-hill like despotism of the Incas. Whatever they may have owed to Old World contacts, they were certainly distinctive enough. Many other civilizations—the Olmecs of Mexico, the Chimus of Peru, and of course, the Mayans of Yucatan, had risen and fallen. In North America, a similar culture, called either "Mound-builders" (so called from the enormous mounds they built) or "Mississippian," had reached practically the same technological level as the Incas or Aztecs about the year 850 A.D. But a few hundred years later it began to break up, under pressure from Plains and Woodland tribes. By the time the Europeans arrived, the Natchez Indians survived as a lone remnant, rather as the Byzantines were of Rome. Interestingly, as the Inca was called the "Son of the Sun," so the chief of the Natchez was titled "The Great Sun."

The North American Indians at the time of the discovery were much more primitive than either their Aztec and Inca contemporaries or their Mississippian predecessors. More settled tribes, such as those in the South and North East, grew pumpkins, beans, corn and squash. Plains Indians, having no horses (none would arrive until the Spanish came), lived sedentary lives in earth lodges nestled along river banks. In the far West, the California Indians lived wretched lives, subsisting primarily off acorns and rabbits (the fires local tribesmen lit to frighten rabbits out of hiding in the Los Angeles area provided that future city's first smog). North Western Indians lived relatively comfortably. These latter were famous for *potlaches*, parties at which the host would give away most of his goods to his guests.

It was a continent teeming with game. Buffalo, deer, elk, rabbit, passenger pigeon, turkey, and many other animals and birds went into the tribesmen's larder, as well as various wild plants, and the four staple crops mentioned above. Further to the South, peanuts, chocolate, and potatoes all were raised. Their subsequent introduction to the rest of the world (from which they were absent) would cause as great a revolution in various Old World countries' diet as importation of European foods and plants would in the Americas.

At any rate, it so happened that, at the time of the discovery, there were no Indian nations capable of real resistance to the Europeans, save the Aztecs and the Incas. The bloodthirstiness of the former and the rigid interior conformity of the latter seriously depleted their ability to defend themselves against any technologically superior culture with which they might come in contact.

AFRICA

The portion of Africa closest to America, West Africa, is naturally the part which would have, via the slave-trade, the closest connection to the New World. Divided among such incessantly warring peoples as the Ashanti, Fante, Dahomey, and Benin, the West African coast was nevertheless a rich source of gold. In 1471, the Portuguese arrived at what they soon called the Gold Coast (present-day Ghana) and in 1482, they built Elmina Castle there, the first of four local forts designed to ensure that other Europeans did not trade in the region. From this depot they hoped to send the gold to Europe, rather than through Moslem North Africa.

The small local states had another interesting custom. Fighting continually as they did, they captured many prisoners. These they would sell as slaves, generally to the larger Moslem states to the North, particularly those in the Sudan. But of course, the change in direction of the gold flow away from these countries reduced their ability to buy slaves. Luckily for the petty coastal chieftains, the discovery of the New World would soon provide a whole new outlet for their wares.

ASIA

But what of Asia, of the glittering Far East which the Portuguese hoped to reach by sea going east, and Columbus by going west? In the 13th Century, *Marco Polo* had reached the court of *Khublai Khan*, Mongol ruler of China. From then on, overland trade and communication between Europe and China grew for about a century, during which time Catholic dioceses were established. Foreigners themselves, the Mongol Emperors of China were friendly to Europeans.

But in 1368, they were driven out of the country, and the native Ming dynasty assumed the throne. Expansionistic, China under the Ming resolved to become a naval power. From 1407 to 1431, Admiral *Cheng Ho* cruised the waters of the Indian Ocean. He visited East African and Arabian ports, and reduced many countries in Southeast Asia to vassals of his Emperor. This was the beginning of the massive emigration of Chinese to those areas, of which their later migration to our West Coast was an eventual product.

But later Emperors did not consolidate the conquests of Cheng Ho. Moreover, the naval interests of China lay to her south and west, not east—where were the fierce Japanese pirates. Although, as earlier suggested, some Chinese may have reached the new world at one time or another, the China of 1492 was not interested in what lay beyond Japan.

Japan herself, in a state of civil war, produced as seamen pirates who were interested only in capturing Chinese ships—thus discouraging Chinese interest in their direction further, and causing them to look westward. The rest of Eastern Asia was too divided to worry about what might lay beyond the Eastern horizon. If the Westerners were interested in Asia, and unable to dislodge the Turks from their control of the traditional overland routes, then they must find a way by sea themselves.

CONCLUSION

This, then, was the situation of the world on August 3, 1492, when Christopher Columbus and his tiny fleet of three ships set sail from Palos Harbor. They did not realize it, nor did any other human on the planet, but the world was set for a major revolution. Those three small ships, the *Niña,* the *Pinta*, and the *Santa Maria,* carried as cargo the future of the world, the civilization of Christendom, and the Catholic Faith. Not only the Americas were to receive these benefits as a result of the voyage, but Asia and Africa too, as

Portuguese efforts to keep up with Spain drove them to pursue their eastern direction more avidly. Further, the cornerstone of our own country was set down that summer day in Spain.

THE FOUNDING OF CATHOLIC AMERICA 1492-1763

GODMOTHER OF THE AMERICAS, ISABEL THE QUEEN

The most obvious thing about medieval monarchy is that like the society over which it presided, it was entirely suffused with Catholicism. The Faith was a living presence in every part of life, and the declared goal of State, as of Church, was the salvation of souls. In the words of historian Catherine Goddard Clarke:

> We have been slowly and deliberately taught that monarchies and kings are bad things, and papal supervision of any kind of government, even over its morals, is a *very* bad thing. The obvious truth, that a bad king can be a bad thing, but that a good king is always a blessedly *good* thing and that the Pope is the divinely constituted guardian of faith and morals for the whole world, is carefully kept from the realization of every school child and man and woman.

Scarcely anyone is ever told any more that France, Spain and Portugal, Poland and Hungary, England and Sweden, all had kings and queens who were saints, and who ruled their lands gloriously and brought untold happiness and well-being to their subjects. (*Our Glorious Popes*, p.59)

But this kind of government was doomed. The decline of feudalism, the emergence of a money economy, and the spirit of irreligion unleashed by the Renaissance all contributed to a this-worldly point of view. Many a king saw in the centralization of power under himself the only way in which his country (and himself) could be truly great. The Church, Guilds, Nobles, Estates—all must be brought under royal control. From this emerged *James I* of England's idea of the "Divine Right of Kings." From it also arose the Scandinavian and English Kings' and North German Princes' determination to rule the Church in their countries as much as the State—which determination allowed the so-called Reformation (i.e., Protestant Revolt) to succeed in those nations. From this also emerged the Modern State apparatus with which we are familiar, whose masters at length either deposed the kings who had called them into existence, or else reduced them to impotence.

This pagan view of the State, that it existed purely for itself and for the exaltation of its ruler, was much in the air in the 15th century. It is remarkable that *Isabel*, though forced at times to centralize, preserved the local liberties as much as was consonant with the good of the realm; she never succumbed to what was then the avant-garde philosophy. She attempted to rule as a good Catholic queen—and that required proper handling of the office we have just described.

Spain Before Isabel

One other bit of stage setting required to explain Isabel's

public career is the state of Spain at the time of her birth. Due to the 750 year long presence of the Moslems in Spain, the county had long been a frontier of Christianity against Islam. In 711, the Moslems triumphed over the Visigothic King Roderick, and overwhelmed the whole country. Under the leadership of a nobleman, Pelagius (Don Pelayo I), a small group of Christians took refuge in the cave of Covadonga in Asturias. From that refuge they sallied forth to do battle with the Infidel. Thus began the eight-century long *Reconquista*, which was ended triumphantly by our heroine in 1492.

That small cave in Asturias was the beginning of the Kingdom of Castile (so called from the castles built against the Moors). Other centers of resistance similarly gave birth to kingdoms as their rulers retook more territory from the Moslems. A French count in the Pyrenees carved out what became the Kingdom of Navarre; another began what became the Kingdom of Aragon, which later absorbed the Frankish province of Barcelona, once restored by Charlemagne to Christendom. Portugal started as a county freed by a Burgundian nobleman. The whole campaign was carried on in this fashion, with some fighting the enemy for one or the other of these kings, and others doing it on their own, like the great hero *Rodrigo de Bivar (a.k.a. El Cid)*. With the expulsion of the Moslems being proclaimed at last a Crusade like the ones raging in Palestine and Prussia, Orders of Knights were formed as they had been in those places—in Santiago, Calatrava, Alcantara, Montesa, Christ, and Aviz. Like their prototypes, the Templars, Hospitallers and Teutonic Knights, the orders were made, by the lands they captured and the castles they built, powers to be reckoned with.

The result of this do-it-yourself reconquest was that each of these kingdoms had wide ly varying institutions and character exceptional even in an age that our own carefully supervised society would consider anarchic. Each province guarded its rights of self-government (the *fueros*) jealously. The nobles were similarly turbulent; the oath of allegiance to the King of Castile by his lords was almost insulting: "To you, who are no better than we are, from us who are as good as you, true faith and allegiance as long as you obey our laws; and if not, no!"

Despite this, Castile still produced some remarkable kings, such as Alfonso X ("the Wise," 1221-1281), and St. Ferdinand III (1201-1252) of whom the great Dom Guéranger writes in *The Liturgical Year*:

> Catholic Spain is personified in her Ferdinand. His mother Berengaria was sister to Blanche, the mother of St. Louis of France. In order to form "the Catholic Kingdom," there was needed one of our Lord's Apostles, St. James the Great; there was needed a formidable trial, the Saracen invasion, which deluged the peninsula; there was needed a chivalrous resistance, which lasted eight hundred years, and by which Spain regained her glory and her freedom. St. Ferdinand is the worthy representative of the brave heroes who drove out the Moors from their fatherland and made her what she is: but he had the virtues of a saint, as well as the courage of a soldier. (Vol. VIII, "Paschal Time," Bk. II, p.630).

St. Ferdinand had in Isabel a worthy descendant, who was always mindful of his example. His efforts restricted the Moors in 1238 to a last remnant of territory, the Kingdom of Granada in the far south of Spain. There they sat, occasionally sending out raiders, but for the most part stagnating in a melancholy fashion well captured by Washington Irving in his *Tales of the Alhambra*.

But this indolence was not to profit the Christians of Spain for another 254 years. Most of St. Ferdinand's successors were not nearly so great. Pedro the Cruel, for instance, while of unpleasant personal habits, was not the man to conquer Granada. But on April 22, 1451, John II, as ineffectual king as ever graced the throne of Castile, was presented by his new wife, Isabel of Portugal (niece of Prince Henry the Navigator), with a daughter. Named after her mother, she would regain for her country the glory of her ancestors, and spread it to lands they had never dreamed of.

Like his contemporary in England, Henry VI, John had been the pawn of rival factions of nobles throughout his reign. Just as the English counterpart of this conflict, the War of the Roses, inflicted untold suffering on Henry's subjects, so too did the Spanish version affect John's. "The Royal Baton," as King John was known, died when his daughter was two years old. He was succeeded by her elder brother, Henry IV, called the "Impotent" or the "Strange."

He was apparently homosexual, and gave his associates free reign–not unlike England's Edward II (1307-1327). Like that unhappy monarch, too, Henry's fecklessness and reliance on favorites led eventually to a revolt by another faction of his nobles, who took umbrage at his mismanagement. They proclaimed the king's heir and younger brother, Alphonso, as king. But when, in 1467, Alphonso died, leaving young Princess Isabel as sole heiress to the realm, the civil war ground to a halt.

How had Isabel fared? Her first eleven years were lived in seclusion with her mother, the dowager Queen; then she arrived at her brother's court, the most corrupt in Europe. When the civil war broke out between her brothers, although she maintained her love for Alphonso, she refused to join the rebellion, preferring to remain in a convent. After Alphonso's death, both sides relied on her as heiress.

Isabel as Queen

In an atmosphere filled with plots and counterplots, Isabel married in 1472 Ferdinand, Crown Prince of Aragon. Two years later, Henry died, leaving Isabel as Queen. Revolts broke out against her; the next few years are an exciting tale of escapes, sieges, and intrigue. But Isabel, Ferdinand at her side, triumphed over her enemies and secured her throne. In 1479, Ferdinand succeeded to the throne of Aragon, and the two largest countries of Spain were united. They would retain separate institutions for many centuries, and so late as the 19th century, the common Spaniards referred to their country as "the Spains." But the emergence of the Spain of today had begun.

As has been noted, the turbulent Spanish nobility were an important force for anarchy. Triumphing over her opponents and safeguarding her throne was an achievement for the Queen in itself. But something had to be done to maintain order and restrain those who during the periods of civil war had taken to robbery. This was, after all, in a day when monarchs had no police force to watch the entire citizenry as we do today. Isabel's solution was typically Spanish, and typically Catholic.

In the Middle Ages, men and women gathered together in all sorts of confraternities. These had as their aim generally both religious and temporal goals. On the religious side, all members were bound to pray for one another, attend Mass together at various feast days, and so on—sometimes one or another of these groups undertook miracle or mystery plays. Our Scapular Confraternities of today are survivals of this kind of thing. More temporally, they often provided for members' burial and support of survivors. Beyond this, though, there could be an almost dizzying number of ends. The Trade and Craft guilds regulated their professions; knightly confraternities did the same in a given district. Then, in areas torn by anarchy and domestic warfare between nobles, confraternities grew up with the goal of maintaining peace. It was an idea that had spread to Spain; various locals on the road to Compostela had formed themselves into confraternities devoted to protection of the pilgrims who wended their way there to venerate the bones of St. James the Great. Defense of such travelers became not merely a civic but a religious duty, with corresponding benefits after death if the job were performed well.

With the breakdown of order in Castile, these confraternities or "Holy Brotherhoods" had declined. But Isabel and her consort revived them in 1476. Companies of the *Santa Hermandad* were formed and subsidized throughout Spain. By 1504, the roads throughout the country were once again safe, and so commerce flourished. The Brotherhoods themselves lasted long enough to play a glorious part in the Peninsular War, acting as a local militia against the French invaders of Napoleon.

But it was not enough merely to apprehend malefactors. They must also be tried—and in remote parts of Castile, where they might be working secretly with the local nobleman to whom judicial power had been delegated—this might be difficult. So Isabel traveled extensively in far away provinces like Extramadura and Andalusia, to sit in judgment over criminals. This was done at great personal risk; but the good of her subjects demanded it, and it was her responsibility as Queen. Here too, she was successful.

The Fall of Granada

The reign of justice restored after long years of labor, she and Ferdinand were now ready to turn their attention to the last remaining Moorish possession—Granada. Although no longer able to threaten most of Spain, the Moors were able to mount bloody raids on the borders. And while they themselves might be quiescent, their co-religionists, the Ottoman Turks, were not. Two years after Isabella was born, Constantinople, the great city of the East and center of the Byzantine

Empire, fell to them. Greece, Serbia, and Bosnia all came under Turkish sway before Isabella took the throne; twenty-two years after her death they would be at the gates of Vienna. Their caravels were already prowling the Mediterranean, a problem which would not be relieved until Isabel's great-grandson, Don John of Austria, defeated them at Lepanto in 1571. As long as any part of Spain lay in Moslem hands—even in those of the enervated Moors—the peninsula could not be truly secure. The last struggle against the Moors began in 1488, and continued until January 1492. The entrance of Ferdinand and Isabella into the Alhambra marked the end of the age-long struggle begun when Don Pelayo emerged from the Covadonga eight centuries before. At last, all Spain was free.

One of the immediate results of this occurrence was the expulsion of the Jews from Spain. This happening has been frequently cited in recent years against the Queen, and it is an important question to address. In order to understand it in context, we must remember that the Spanish Jews had, from the first invasion by the Moors back in 711, collaborated closely with the Moslem invaders, who were, after all, also a Semitic people. This was considered an act of betrayal by the Spanish. During the long years of Moorish tyranny, Jews often served under them as governors of the Christian populace; Jewish culture in Spain flourished, Toledo and Cordova in particular becoming centers of Hebrew thought and learning. While such collaboration is easily understood, so too is the resentment toward it. When an occupying force is at last dislodged from a nation's territories, those who collaborated with the occupiers—as Pierre Laval and Vikdun Quisling found out after World War II—often do not fare very well.

But where 20th century rulers faced with large ethnic minorities might launch genocide against them, as did the

Turks with the Armenians and the Nazis with the Gypsies, Jews, and Poles (or else "ethnic cleansing" as the Serbian Communists call it), Isabel had no such desire. She feared possible future collaboration of the Jews with Moslems–and she had not defeated restive nobles, brigands, and the Granada Moors to see it all lost to Turks. But as a Catholic she would certainly not want them wantonly executed. What, then, to do?

At this point, in order to explain her motivations, a few points must be made about her and her contemporaries' understanding of Catholicism. They believed Our Lord's words "Unless a man be baptized of water and the Holy Ghost, he shall not enter the Kingdom of God," and "Unless a man eat my body and drink my blood, he shall not have life in him." They agreed with Pope Boniface VIII in his bull, *Unam Sanctam,* that "it is absolutely necessary to the salvation of every human creature to be subject to the Roman Pontiff." This is why the Protestant Henry of Navarre (later Henry IV of France) said in regard to his conversion to Catholicism, "the ministers say that I can save my soul as a Catholic, the priests that I cannot save it as a Protestant. Therefore I can surely be saved as a Catholic." Without this understanding, none of the Queen's actions with regard to the Jews or to the Guanches and Indians (of whom more presently) can be understood.

For like her Savior, she did not desire the death of sinners, but that they should live. She wished that all of her subjects might be members of the Catholic Church, outside of which she believed there was no salvation. If the Jews would convert (for Church law forbade her to force them to do so) they would be given all the privileges and rights of ordinary Spaniards. If not, they were a security risk, and must go. In the event, at most 160,000 left. Many of these, interestingly enough, were picked up by Ottoman vessels and brought to Thessalonica and Constantinople, in which city the anniversary of their arrival was celebrated in 1992. Others went to North Africa, and still others to the Netherlands where, unhampered by the Church's laws against usury, they laid the foundations for that country's capitalist economy and eventual financial prowess. Those who converted, however, soon reached the heights of Spanish society. Many became bishops and nobles and high courtiers; St. Teresa of Avila, for example, was part Jewish.

The Discovery of America

But 1492 was not only concerned with the fall of Granada and the expulsion of the Jews: as every American schoolchild knows, it was the year that "Columbus sailed the ocean blue." In so doing, he opened up a new world, filled with new problems in administration.

Nevertheless, Isabel was not completely unfamiliar with colonies. In 1404, the Castilians had begun the conquest of the Canary Islands, which would not be completed until 1496. Their native inhabitants, a blonde, blue-eyed people called the Guanches, were and are something of a mystery. Fierce warriors, they are claimed by some anthropologists to have been pure Cro-Magnons, by some linguists to have spoken a language related to the equally mysterious North African Tuareg. However all that may be, they certainly were monotheists, extremely primitive, and dogged opponents.

In 1472, Pope Sixtus IV called the Christian powers involved in the Canaries (primarily Castile) to make every effort to convert them. Five years later, discovering that many of the Guanches were being sold into slavery (an institution only just being revived among Christians), Ferdinand and Isabella issued this decree:

> Know that we have heard that some persons have
> brought some natives of the Canary Islands, and, by the

will of the lord of those islands and other persons, have
sold them and divided them out among themselves as
slaves, though some are Christians, and others on their
way to converting to our Holy Catholic Faith. This is a
great disservice to God and to us and is detrimental to
our Holy Catholic Faith, and it would be a great burden
on our consciences to consent to it, because it would
lead to no one wishing to convert to the Holy Faith.
(Quoted in Warren Carroll, *Isabel of Spain*, p.120).

Nor were they content to let their decree sit; they dispatched two trusted advisors to the Canaries to ensure com-
pliance.

A 1490 uprising on the Canary island of Gomera was
suppressed by Governor Pedro de Vera with great ferocity,
most of the inhabitants being killed or sold as slaves, despite
the fact that many of the survivors were Christian. When
word of this outrage reached Isabel and Ferdinand, they
moved into action. Although many of the men of Gomera
had been implicated in the revolt, those who had been were
dead; the women and children were not involved, and being
Christian had full civil rights. They could not be slaves.
Five million maravedis (Spanish currency) were taken from
the Governor as security for the transportation of the
Gomerans back to their homes from wherever they had been
sold. This order was scrupulously carried out. Never again
would an attempt be made to enslave the Canary Islanders,
and they settled down to become loyal Spaniards.

The result has been that culturally, the Islands are almost identical to Spain. Still, the Canarios have a much higher
incidence of blue-eyed blondes then does most of Spain, and
on Gomera the strange Guanche "whistling-language" used
to communicate from hill-top to hill-top is still used. Apart
from exporting the canary bird, Canario settlers went to various spots in Latin America. Some of the oldest families in

San Antonio, Texas are descended from the Canarios, and the *Isleños* of St. Bernard Parish, Louisiana, settled there by the Spanish in the 1770s, still preserve old Canario folk songs and dialect. But the Canaries played one other great part in Spanish history; they were the base from which Francisco Franco launched his war against the anti-clerical, leftist government in 1936. As they were the first part of Spain's overseas empire, so today they are the last.

What all of this meant was that when Columbus discovered America, Ferdinand and Isabella already had a plan for dealing with colonial peoples. Though he hoped to find gold in the East in order to pay for the attempted conquest of Granada by Isabel and Ferdinand, when Columbus presented his project to the king and queen, it was not in terms of finding new routes to China, nor of proving the world round (which educated opinion believed in any case). It was to win souls for Christ. Let it not be forgotten that the militant Catholicism, encompassing within it the desire to conquer the world for Christ, built up over eight centuries of struggle, needed an outlet. The Portuguese had found one; starting with Isabel's uncle, Prince Henry the Navigator, they had voyaged down the West Coast of Africa. By the time a half-century had passed after Isabel's death, the Portuguese would have settlements all along the Indian Ocean, from Mozambique to Indonesia. While this effort gave rise to many abuses (as every human endeavor does) it allowed St. Francis Xavier alone the opening to baptize 3,000,000 in the countries he visited; and he would have many colleagues to follow his example. To this day, the Church in Japan, China and all the countries which touch the Indian Ocean owe their origin to these Portuguese efforts; the surnames of thousands of Catholic Sri Lankans, Indians, Malaysians, Pakistanis, Bangladeshis, and Indonesians are further proof.

It should not be surprising then that the same fervor

could be found in Spanish hearts. After Columbus' discovery, in 1493, Pope Alexander VI divided the non-Christian world between the Spanish and the Portuguese. To the latter was given responsibility for the evangelization and civilizing of the East Indies and Brazil; to the former, the same with regard to the Americas excepting Brazil. The words of the Pope's Bull, *Inter Caetera*, reflect well the spirit in which the great work was undertaken:

> Wherefore, as becomes Catholic kings and princes, after earnest consideration of all matters, especially the rise and spread of the Catholic faith, as was the fashion of your ancestors, kings of renowned memory, you have purposed with the favor of divine clemency to bring under your sway the said mainlands and islands with their residents and inhabitants and to bring them to the Catholic faith. Hence, heartily commending in the Lord this your holy and praiseworthy purpose, and desirous that it be duly accomplished, and that the name of our Savior be carried into those regions, we exhort you very earnestly in the Lord and by your reception of holy baptism, whereby you are bound to our apostolic commands, and by the bowels of the mercy of Our Lord Jesus Christ, enjoin strictly, that inasmuch as with eager zeal for the true faith you design to equip and dispatch this expedition, you purpose also, as is your duty, to lead the peoples dwelling in those islands and countries to embrace the Christian religion; nor at any time let dangers or hardships deter you therefrom, with the stout hope and trust in your hearts that Almighty God will further your undertakings.

Within the lifetime of Isabella, only the Island of Hispaniola was colonized. But there was laid the foundation of Spanish America which today extends culturally from Tierra Del Fuego to San Francisco Bay and Southern Colorado. The spirit of the legislation she and Ferdinand drafted

for this first American possession has been well captured by
historian C. H. Haring:

> The Papal Bull of 1493, which gave to the kings of
> Castile dominion over the Indies, imposed one supreme
> obligation: to spread the gospel and draw the pagans into
> the Church of Christ; and Isabella to the day of her death
> regarded the welfare of the American natives as a major
> responsibility. When, therefore, the new governor, Nicolás
> de Ovando, came out to America in 1502, he was in-
> structed by Isabella to assure the native chiefs that they
> and their people were under the crown's special protec-
> tion. They might go in entire freedom about the island,
> and no one was to rob them or harm them in any way,
> under severe penalties. They were to pay tribute only as
> the rest of the king's subjects. Only in the royal service in
> mines or on public works might they be compelled to
> labor. These orders were followed to the letter. But left to
> themselves, the Indians refused to work....They with-
> drew from all association with the colonists, with results
> that from the European point of view were disastrous.
> Within a few months Governor Ovando wrote to Spain
> protesting that the only effect was the falling off of trib-
> ute, lack of labor, and inability to carry forward the work
> of conversion to Christianity.

> The sovereigns replied with the famous orders of
> March and December 1503, which legalized the forced
> labor of free Indians but attempted at the same time to
> protect them from uncontrolled exploitation. The na-
> tives must be made to work, if necessary, on buildings
> and farms and in the mines, but in moderation and for
> reasonable wages. At the same time, to ensure their be-
> ing civilized, they must be gathered into villages, under
> the administration of a patron or protector, and provided
> with a school and a missionary priest. Each adult Indian
> was to have a house and land which he might not alien-
> ate. Intermarriage of Spaniards and Indians was also to

be encouraged. And in everything they were to be treated "as free persons, for such they are." Only cannibal Indians from neighboring islands if taken in war might be sold into slavery. (*The Spanish Empire in America*, pp.39-40).

The *encomienda*, as this system was called, was intended to spread the Faith among the Indians; the first requirement for the *encomiendero* as the patron was called, was the instruction and baptism of the Indians entrusted to him. In practice, the system did not work well, and giving rise to many abuses was denounced by **Bartolome de Las Casas** to the Crown in 1517, after which it was abolished. After that, Indians in the Spanish territories were to be subject to the king himself, and live under their own chiefs or *caiciques*. Some of these, like Mexico's Princes of Tlaxcala or Peru's Marquesses of Oropesa, were to become great noblemen in their own right. The Tlaxcalans, for example, by order of Charles V, were given the title "Don," exempted from taxes, and were permitted to ride horses; they played an important part in the settlement of the Philippines, Northern Mexico, and New Mexico. It was not until Latin American independence dawned that the new centralizing governments destroyed Indian autonomy. But all of these developments were far off when Isabel died in 1504.

The Queen's Legacy

What is important in this context is the Queen's motivation in her legislation regarding the Indians. For Ferdinand and Isabel, the American territories were not Spanish colonies, actually, but separate realms. Eventually, after the conquests of Mexico and Peru, their concept of governance was carried out under their successors. So the King of Spain was in the end king really of the Spains: that is, Castile, Aragon, Navarre, the Canaries, New Spain (Mexico, Central America,

the Spanish West Indies, the Philippines, Florida and the US
South West, as well as Guam and the Marianas), Peru (including Chile), New Granada (Colombia, Ecuador, Venezuela, and Panama), and Rio de la Platt (Argentina, Bolivia,
Paraguay, and Uruguay). Each of these "Spains" were in
theory equal, none subordinate to the other, but all subject
to the same king. Subjects in each of these countries were
full citizens if they were Catholic and spoke Spanish. Obviously, theory and practice, during the long centuries of Spanish rule, were rarely completely in accord. But the Spanish
were much more humane in the overall to the Indians than
were the English. This is due in no small part to the initial
tenor of Isabel's legislation on their behalf.

Isabel was fully Catholic in both her public and private
personae. As Queen she believed in the divinely bestowed
responsibilities Spain's essentially sacral political order had
endowed her with. As Queen it was part of her royal duties
to found churches and monasteries, and to give gifts to already existing ones. The furtherance of the Faith was a major motif of her foreign and colonial policies. The Orders of
Calatrava, Santiago, Montesa, and Alcantara were still possessed of enormous lands, despite the ending of the Moorish
war. So powerful were they, and so fractious their membership, that they could have become a threat to the Crown. To
forestall this from happening, but to also maintain their integrity as religious orders, she united their Grand Masterships
with the Kingship. In this way royal patronage bolstered them
and they supported the Crown.

But Isabel's religion was not merely public:

> Isabel has been called a mystic who managed to lead
> the life of a contemplative in the midst of an absorbing
> career, but there was nothing in her mysticism of that
> dreamy quietism from the east that denies the claims of
> reality and takes refuge in a subjective passivity. Like all

the great western mystics–like Saint Teresa, like Saint Catherine of Siena, like Saint Ignatius Loyola–she was acutely conscious of the problems of this world and of her duties toward them, and like them she found in prayer the motive power for large and heroic actions. In every crisis she humbly laid her difficulties at the feet of God; but having appealed to Him with all confidence, she proceeded to do her part with an energy that would have commanded the admiration of those less articulate Yankee farmers whose motto was, "Trust God, and keep your powder dry" (Walsh, *op. cit.*, p.246).

Despite the pressures which surrounded her continually, she kept both her personal devotion and her private and public morality intact, for which reason Washington Irving called her "one of the purest and most beautiful characters in the pages of history."

THE CONQUISTADORES

Coming as it did at the end of the long struggle with Islam, the Spanish colonization of the Americas was undertaken in the same manner as the *Reconquista,* and before that, the Crusades. As with those struggles, the story of the Conquest of the New World sees the highest motives mixed with some dreadful actions. But that has always been true of any human endeavor which has as its declared goal anything higher than basic survival. It is important to remember that the Conquistadore had much the same attitudes as did the medieval knight; that is how we must understand them–as later flowers of chivalry. What Leon Gautier said of their crusading forerunners is true of the Conquistadores also:

> The faith of these rude warriors, that faith which was so precise, had nothing namby-pamby in it: nothing *dilettante* or effeminate. We have not to do with the little sugar-plums of certain contemporary devotion–but with

a good and frank wild-honey. It is a grosser but loyal
Catholicism (*Chivalry*, p.27).

It is certainly true that in their number were unscrupu-
lous and greedy men—like Francisco Pizarro. But over all,
they were as idealistic and practical a group of men as any
who have ever set out on a goal higher than themselves. We
cannot look at all of them, but we will examine a few of the
most important.

Christopher Columbus

We do not usually think of Columbus as a Conquistadore,
but it was he who opened the way. An ancestor of his had
been aboard the boat which received the dying Bl. Raymond
Lully, when that mystic and missionary was stoned by a North
African mob in Tunis in 1316. Lully's last words were to say
that there lay another continent beyond the sea, and to admonish his hearers to send missionaries there to save souls.
This account was preserved in the young Columbus' family
and made a great impression on him.

Born in Genoa, Columbus went to sea at 14, sailing as
far away as Iceland. He eventually made his way to Portugal
to study at the school of Prince Henry the Navigator, doubtless receiving not only navigational skills but also the crusading and missionary zeal of the Knights of Christ who ran the
school. With them, as we have seen, he sailed to the Gold
Coast of Africa. He attempted to interest the Kings of Portugal, England, and France in his idea of sailing around the
world to Asia; in this he failed. Luckily, Fr. Mendez, the
Queen's confessor, took an interest in him and his work, and
attained an audience with Ferdinand and Isabel. They were
not very receptive at first. But the fall of Granada gave them
leisure for other projects. Columbus received their backing,
and the New World was duly discovered.

Columbus' landing on October 12, 1492 was significant in innumerable ways. Not least of these is the fact that it is the feast day of Our Lady of the Pillar. This commemorates the very first apparition of Our Lady, which occurred while she yet lived. St. James the Apostle, having had very little success with converting the Spaniards, was about to go back to Palestine. But in Saragossa (Caesarea Augusta, as it was in Roman times), the Blessed Virgin appeared to him, and assured him that, if he stayed, the Spanish would one day become a great Catholic people. He did, and they did, eventually revering St. James as their patron and treasuring his relics at Santiago de Compostela.

At any rate, much discouraged, and with his crew near mutiny, Columbus agreed to turn back to Spain if land was not sighted by sundown on the feast of Our Lady of the Pillar; doubtless he felt much like St. James. Like St. James, his perseverance was rewarded, and America discovered. He would make a total of four voyages to America, founding the first permanent settlement by Europeans in the Americas–Santo Domingo, on the island of Hispaniola. His career was difficult, and he faced much opposition, from enemies at court, from disobedient subordinates, and from the Indians the latter provoked. Many of the slanders his enemies made against him are used today as well by enemies of the Faith.

But the truth about Columbus is that his primary goal was to convert the Asians (as he thought the Indians to be) to Catholicism. He was very pious, being in fact a Third Order Franciscan and buried in the Franciscan habit. Although his enemies at last had him sent home to Spain in chains in 1504, he was not embittered. Indeed, he offered to set sail again, and to spend his last possession on what would have been his crowning voyage: an attempt to regain the Holy Sepulcher from the Infidels. But it was not to be, and death claimed him in 1506. He was even proposed for Sainthood; a storm of opposition from Protestant and other quarters stymied this attempt in 1892–not unlike that which beset his memory in 1992. It really does not matter, however. The day of his discovery is kept as a national holiday, Columbus Day, in the United States, the Bahamas, Belize, Chile, Colombia, Costa Rica, the Dominican Republic, Ecuador, El Salvador, Guatemala, Honduras, Mexico, Paraguay, Spain, Uruguay, and Venezuela. Thus the father of the Americas has, indirectly, been responsible for the erection of the Feast of Our Lady of the Pillar into a legal holiday in 16 countries. Given Columbus' character, it is an accomplishment which doubtless would have pleased him more than merely discovering a new continent.

Hernando Cortez

Ferdinand and Isabel's daughter, Juana, married in her turn the handsome Philip of Burgundy, himself the son of Maximilian I, the gallant and chivalrous Holy Roman Emperor. Unfortunately, Juana went mad after her husband's premature death; their son Charles I therefore succeeded his grandfather, Ferdinand, when the latter died in 1516. Having already been ruler of Burgundy and The Netherlands when his father died, he found himself ruler of a vast empire in the New World. The major islands of the West Indies were being colonized, and the shores of Mexico and Central America were being explored. In 1518, word was brought back to Havana of the Aztec Empire of Mexico. The next year, two great events happened: Charles I succeeded his grandfather Maximilian as Holy Roman Emperor (thus picking up the Habsburg territories in Central Europe and the responsibility of dealing with the Protestant Revolt–Martin Luther began his activities in 1517–and the Turks); and an expedition was fitted out in Havana to bring the Aztecs into Spain's dominion in accordance with the mandate of

Alexander VI. The man chosen to lead it was Hernando Cortez.

Headstrong and impetuous, Cortez had the courage and daring necessary for such a quest. Landing at San Juan de Uloa near Vera Cruz on April 21, 1519, he had few troops; 600 infantry, 16 cavalry, 13 cross-bowmen, and 14 cannon were the entirety of his force. As it turned out, however, he had arrived at precisely the time and place predicted by Quetzalcoatl; the Aztecs did not move immediately against him as a result. This delay allowed him to make contact with the Tlaxcalans and other Indian subjects of the Aztecs. Tired of long years of seeing their handsomest and most beautiful young men and women sacrificed in their thousands to the Aztec gods, they joined the Spanish. This turned the tide; by 1521, Mexico was in Cortez' hands.

This did not last long, however, for a man of Cortez' nature could not get along well with superiors. He was eventually removed from office, and returned to Spain in 1540, dying in Seville seven years later. His was not as sterling a character as Columbus'. But he was a friend to the clergy; it is also notable that he named his first town, Vera Cruz, after the True Cross. If he was at times cruel and barbaric in his treatment of the Aztecs, it should be remembered that his Indian allies presented him with innumerable accounts of Aztec atrocities; his reaction was not unlike that of the American soldiers who liberated the German concentration camps in 1945.

Heaven, however, gave its sign of approval to the conquest. Ten years afterwards, Our Lady appeared dressed as an Aztec princess to the Indian Juan Diego, at the hill of Tepeyac outside Mexico City. She told him that she wanted a shrine built there in her honor, and that he was to tell the bishop of this request. The bishop demanded proof; this Our Lady provided, when she told Juan to gather roses on the hillside—a difficult feat in a Mexican winter. But there they were; he gathered them in his *tilma* (a sort of poncho) and brought them to the cathedral. Releasing them from his cloak, all were struck by the image on it—that image known to us as Our Lady of Guadelupe. Reaction was immediate; by the time Cortez left Mexico, nine million Mexican Indians had converted. This came about at the very time that kings and princes in Europe were tearing their people out of Christendom, and taking total control of their realms. So, at least in terms of numbers, what was lost in the Old World was made up in the New.

Hernando De Soto and Francisco Coronado

De Soto (1500-1542), discoverer of the Mississippi, was a Knight of the Order of Santiago and Governor of Cuba. Determined to advance the cause of Christ on "the Northern Rim of Christendom" (as the Spaniards were already beginning to call North America), he landed in Florida, and marched through that state, Georgia, Alabama, and Mississippi. Reaching the river which gives its name to the last state, he explored it up as far as the Ohio. Many skirmishes were fought with hostile Indians; fever claimed De Soto, and he was buried in the Great River he had discovered.

Michael V. Gannon in his *The Cross in the Sand* sums up De Soto's character very well:

> Although it is recorded that De Soto was not above the use of deception in his dealings with the Indians, nor averse to reducing them to slavery when it suited his purposes, to his credit it is also recorded that he sometimes assisted the priests in instructing Indian chiefs and tribesmen in Christianity. On one such occasion....De Soto fashioned and raised a towering pine-tree Cross at the town of Casqui on the western bank of the Mississippi, and proclaimed to the Indians of the place: "This

was He who had made the sky and the earth and man in His own image. Upon the tree of the Cross He suffered to save the human race, and rose from the tomb on His third day... and, having ascended into heaven, was there to receive with open arms all who would be converted to Him."

Gannon goes on to evaluate De Soto as:

> A brave soldier, a man of invincible spirit and high resolve, a rude but earnest missionary... (pp.8-9).

Francisco de Coronado (1500-1553), while De Soto was exploring the South-East, set off for the South West. Like De Soto, he was led on by Indian reports of wealthy cities which, mirage-like, seemed to recede ever further into the distance. Having left Mexico in 1540, he wintered among the Pueblo Indians, and then set off after reports of "Quivira." He moved ever northward through modern day Texas, Oklahoma, Kansas, and Nebraska. But at last, discouraged, he gave up and returned to Mexico City. But one item was left behind in Kansas, to be discovered in 1886: a Spanish sword from Coronado's expedition, inscribed with the name of its owner, Juan Gallegos, and on the blade these words– "Do not draw me without right. Do not sheathe me without honor." Here at once is summed up the essential chivalry of the Conquistadores.

Pedro De Menendez

Despite all of these and other explorers, Spain failed to establish a permanent settlement in the present United States. Meanwhile, Emperor Charles V, worn out with fighting the Protestants and the Turks, abdicated his thrones in 1555. To his brother, Ferdinand I, he gave the Empire and the Habsburg Austrian lands. To his son, Philip II, he gave Spain and its rapidly growing overseas empire.

To that empire and its shipping, English and French Protestant pirates constituted a grave threat. When a band of the latter established a nest at Ft. Caroline (present-day Jacksonville, FL), the better to menace Cuba with, Philip resolved on action. His military commander, Pedro de Menendez, was given a royal commission to clear out the pirates, and to found a Spanish town in the area which would serve to prevent the same thing happening again. On September 8, 1565, the town of St. Augustine was founded on its present site. The next month, the pirates of Ft. Caroline were wiped out. The first part of Menendez's job was completed.

The second, securing the safety and prosperity of St. Augustine, would take longer. Indeed, it would not be until 1606 that the town was on a firm foundation. But in the meantime, the most important thing was to secure a steady supply not only of colonists (hard to obtain–living in Spain at that time was very pleasant, and few wished to leave), but of missionaries. Menendez wrote a letter to the Spanish Jesuits, imploring them to send some of their number:

> They [the Indians] ask me to make them Christian as we are, and I have told them that I am waiting for your Honors, so you can make wordlists, and quickly learn their language, and then tell them how they are to be Christians, and enlighten them that if they are not they are serving and having as their Lord the most evil creature of the world, which is the devil, who is deceiving them, and that if they are Christian, they will be enlightened and serve Our Lord, who is Chief of Heaven and earth; and then, being happy and content, they will be our true brothers, and we will give them whatever we may have.

Menendez did not live to see his vision become a reality. But it did. Eventually, although Spain's actual colonizing efforts produced only St. Augustine and Pensacola in Florida, her missionaries—Jesuit and Franciscan—Catholicized northern Florida, Western and coastal Georgia, and coastal South Carolina. Like the Princes of Tlaxcala and the Marquises of Oropesa whom we have already encountered, the caiciques of the twenty-seven converted tribes were direct vassals of the king, with whom some corresponded familiarly. Indeed, because the missionaries reduced the Indian languages to writing, they wrote one another, long before the Pilgrims ever saw Plymouth Rock. In truth, much of Spanish power in the present US rested on the shoulders of the mission padres, at whom we shall now take a closer look.

THE MISSIONARIES

There can be no doubt that the Spanish missionaries in the US were much assisted in their efforts by many miracles, such as the one at Guadalupe. Most spectacular and best known of these is the experience of *Venerable Maria de Agreda* (1602-1665). At that time, the first Franciscan missionaries reached the tribes of West Texas and Eastern New Mexico. Much to their surprise, the Padres found that a few of the tribes were already aware of Catholicism, knew its doctrines, and asked for Baptism. When asked how they knew, they replied that they had been taught by a lady in blue. Several of the Friars returned to Spain, and found Maria de Agreda, head of a convent of nuns who wore blue habits; she claimed to have bilocated to the New World to instruct Indians there. Questioned in detail about the appearances and customs of those she allegedly had taught, she described to them perfectly the tribes they had just left. The account is commemorated in a picture at the Cathedral of Fort Worth, Texas. But why did she go to those tribes, rather than others? Good will, one must suppose. At any rate, one who was inspired by her example was the Apostle of California, *Bl.*

Junipero Serra.

A professor of Bl. Raymond Lully's philosophy, he followed the example of his mentor, whom we met dying in view of one of Columbus' forebears, and went to California, eventually founding the string of Missions which were the start of its modern culture. Upon his arrival in 1771 at the future site of Mission San Antonio de Padua (near present day Jolon) in central California, he immediately unloaded a bell from a mule, hung it on a tree, and rang it. All the while he shouted "O ye gentiles! Come to the holy church!" His associates reminded him that there were neither Indians nor a church about, to which he replied that he just wanted to "give vent to my desires that this bell might be heard all over the World!" But shortly thereafter, an old Indian woman came into the camp, asking to be baptized. The padres were quite shocked, seeing that there had been no one there to explain the sacrament or its need to the Indians. But the woman explained that her father had told her about a man who appeared to him four times, explaining to him the doctrines of Catholicism. Satisfying their questions, she was forthwith baptized.

Missionaries as Colonizers

Just as the settling of Florida was primarily achieved by evangelizing the Indians rather than bringing over Spanish colonists, so too with the rest of Spanish North America. Thirty-three years after St. Augustine was founded, Juan de Oñate set off with a group of 400 colonists for New Mexico. He founded the city of Santa Fe, then as now, capital of the province. Then as now, Santa Fe was surrounded by Indian Pueblos. Rather than try to destroy them, as the English might later, the Spanish Franciscans set to work converting them. They taught them the Creation story by having them act it out; they had them perform their dances in honor of Our

Lord and Lady, and the Saints. So Spanish and Indians lived side-by-side; each retaining their own ways, but sharing a common Faith.

It was not until 1698 that Spain occupied Texas. With that first band came *Fr. Massenet.* While soldiers and Canary Islanders were founding the town of San Antonio, Massenet and those padres who followed him were founding missions, of which the Alamo is certainly the most famous. Two years later, *Eusebio Kino, S.J.*, entered Arizona, to found San Xavier del Bac near Tucson. So firmly did he and his successors plant the Catholic Faith among the Pima Indians of the area, that when San Xavier del Bac lay abandoned for a century and a half, the Pimas kept it in perfect condition until the Jesuits returned.

In 1769, Bl. Junipero Serra began California. The founding of the twenty-one California missions did not cease until the last, San Francisco Solano in Sonoma, was opened in 1821. There were in addition, four *presidios* (forts), two towns (Los Angeles and San Jose) and many ranchos. Obviously, until they were secularized by the Mexican government in 1831, the missions and their Indian inhabitants were the bulk of Spanish California.

All of this achievement was not without its cost in blood. Eighty-three Spanish missionaries were martyred for the Faith by hostile Indians or by the English in the course of their work, starting with *Fr. Juan de Padilla, O.F.M.* in the fall of 1542, and ending with *Fr. Antonio Diaz de Leon,* killed by Texan-American frontiersmen for his religion in 1834.

Yet this was merely the tip of the missionary iceberg in Spanish America, and far from the most important region. We cannot do more than mention the Jesuit *Reducciones* of Paraguay, where from 1607 to 1768 the padres ruled over a veritable mission state. Even an enemy of the Church, Voltaire, could say of them:

...they had arrived at what is perhaps the highest degree of civilization to which it is possible to lead a young people... Laws were there respected, morals were pure, a happy brotherhood bound men together, the useful arts and even some of the more pleasing sciences flourished; there was abundance everywhere.

The Dominican *Vasco de Quiroga* in the 1530s established a similar commonwealth in his chain of missions among the Tarascan Indians around Lake Patzcuaro in Mexico's Michoacan State. Many of the crafts he taught are still practiced by the Tarascans, who continue to venerate his name. There were many more examples throughout the Spanish Americas.

THE SPANISH ACHIEVEMENT

By 1763, the Spanish possessions in the New World constituted an incredible achievement. Stretching from the frontier in North America–"the Northern Rim of Christendom," Spanish rule continued down through Mexico and Central America, through the Andes mountains to the plains of the Pampas, ending at Patagonia, and hemming in Portuguese Brazil (where a similar achievement had been undertaken). Taking in every conceivable kind of environment, it was an area of peace for over 300 years, despite a very small military force. After the conquest, the main areas under Spanish control developed a life as advanced as Europe at the same time. Churches, monasteries, fine houses and public buildings, universities and the arts all flourished. To this day, although the University of Mexico City is ultramodern in style, it owes its foundation to Pontifical and Royal charters issued in the 1550's; the monumental cathedral of Guadalajara boasts a statue of Our Lady of the Roses given by Emperor Charles V, and eleven elegant side-altars donated by Ferdinand VII.

Many more tangible examples of royal favor dot Latin America. Indians who had acquired degrees in Spanish-American universities went back to the mother-country to teach. The wealth from gold and silver mines and from ranchos led to great beauty in the cities of the New World. But above all, the influence of the Church produced Saints. Not just martyrs, but miracle-working contemplatives, just as she had in Europe. *Ss. Turibius, Rose, Juan Macias*, and *Martin de Porres* (himself of Spanish, Indian, and Black blood) all lived in 17th century Lima, just as *St Peter Claver* attended to the needs of Black slaves in Cartagena.

The Peoples of Spanish America

Most appointed officials in the Americas were *peninsulares*, natives of Spain. To prevent the growth of a native oligarchy which might one day take over control of the colonies (which in fact happened in the English colonies), political power was generally in the hands of peninsulares, who nevertheless constituted a small minority of the population.

The *criollos* (whence comes our word Creole) were the native-born Spaniards. Few rose to high position in the Spanish administration, but many were very wealthy. Quite a number bore Spanish titles of nobility.

Mestizos were people of mixed white and Indian blood. They tended to form a sort of middle-class, working as artisans, farmers, and foot soldiers. There were very many more of them than of the criollos or peninsulares.

Indians were governed by their own rulers, as we saw earlier.

The Blacks had been imported originally as slaves. In the beginning, Indians were used as cheap labor (as we use immigrants in factories). But mines and fields took a heavy toll. Their major advocate, *Fr. Bartolome de Las Casas*, had

come to the New World in 1500. To relieve them of their
burdens, he called on the Spanish to import Blacks instead.
Since, as has been mentioned, the slave marts of the Guinea
Coast had few customers at the time, prices were low. Thus
began the importation of African slaves to the New World.
Obviously, Spanish, Portuguese, French, Dutch, and English
all took part in the trade. But it should be emphasized that
the influence of the Church in Catholic countries produced
a much more humane version of the system than that which
prevailed in Dutch or English possessions. Among the Spanish, there were protective regulations regarding housing, food,
work, and punishment. Slaves could choose their own wives
and change masters if they could find their own buyer. They
were able to purchase themselves at the lowest possible rate;
so it was that by the end of the 18th century, black freedmen
outnumbered slaves in the Spanish colonies. Needless to say,
the law required masters to bring their slaves into the Faith
and assist them in observing it.

Government

As mentioned, the King of Spain was independently king
of each of his Viceroyalties. To assist him in this, he maintained in Spain the Council of the Indies, which carried on
the day-to-day running of affairs in the Americas, subject to
the King's approval.

In New Spain, Peru, New Granada, and Rio de La Plata,
the king was represented by the Viceroy, whose authority in
his territory was theoretically as supreme as the King's. But
every three years, a Visitor was sent by the Council of the
Indies to audit his administration, and recommend improve-
ments or personnel changes if necessary. In addition, each
Viceroyalty possessed an *audencia*, which acted as the
Viceroy's Council. The Viceroyalties were further divided
into Captaincy-Generals and Provinces, presided over by

Captains-General and Governors. Each major city had in addition a *cabildo*, a sort of city council, on which criollos could sit, and which was responsible for most of the every-day acts of administration.

The Spanish Achievement in Latin America

To put it bluntly, all of Latin America save Portuguese-speaking Brazil and French-speaking Haiti owe everything of value they possess to Spain. Religion, language, culture, learning, their very existence, all of this came from the mother country. Considering how few Spaniards actually came to the Americas, this is really amazing. Unfortunately, much of this legacy has been destroyed by many of the post-independence governments in Latin America, often with the assistance or at the urging of, sadly, these United States. This is particularly tragic, since our debt to Spain is almost as great.

The Spanish Achievement in the United States

While, as we shall see in the next chapter, the unique civilization the Spanish developed in Florida was destroyed by the English, the foundations they planted in California, Texas, New Mexico, and Arizona survived to be taken advantage of by the Americans in their Westward expansion. Numbers alone are intriguing: SOUTH CAROLINA: 1 mission, 2 presidios; NORTH CAROLINA: 2 missions, 3 presidios; VIRGINIA: 1 mission; ALABAMA: 1 mission, 4 presidios; Mississippi: 2 presidios; TENNESSEE: 2 presidios; ARKANSAS: 2 presidios; LOUISIANA: 6 presidios; MISSOURI: 3 presidios; GEORGIA: 31 missions, 6 presidios; FLORIDA: 96 missions, 22 presidios; TEXAS: 47 missions, 14 presidios; NEW MEXICO: 58 missions, 5 presidios; ARIZONA: 16 missions, 5 presidios; CALIFORNIA: 21 missions, 5 presidios. Intrepid explorers that they were, the Spanish linked many of the missions with trails, such as those extending from Sonoma,

California to San Diego; from Santa Fe to El Paso, and thence
to Chihuahua; and the one which linked Nagadoches to San
Antonio and Laredo. Each of these was inevitably called *El
Camino Real*: "The King's Highway," along which traveled
both padres and soldiers of the king.

But there is more than this; notice the proportions of
missions to presidios. Consider also how few Spanish settlers
came here. Apart from St. Augustine and Pensacola in Florida,
the major towns the Spanish settled were Los Angeles and
San Jose, California; Tucson, Arizona; Taos and Santa Fe,
New Mexico; and San Antonio, El Paso, Laredo, and
Nagadoches, Texas. The Spanish were not interested in destroying the native peoples, but in making them Catholics
and Spaniards, even while retaining the best parts of their
indigenous cultures. How different indeed from English and
subsequent American policy! The important thing to remember is that, apart from the initial conquest, Spain's rule of her
American colonies was less dependent upon force than upon
religion, culture, and the rule of law. That is certainly a description of good government. We shall see in subsequent
chapters if anything better replaced her rule.

When the Spanish Habsburgs ended with the death of
Charles II in 1700, the throne passed to Louis XIV of France's
grandson, *Philip V* (1683-1746), thus starting the line of
the Spanish Bourbons, who hold the throne of Spain today.
A war was fought over this, the War of Spanish Succession.
But the reign of the Spanish Bourbons introduced the "mod-
ernizing," centralizing methods of Louis XIV into the Spains.
This tendency came to a head under ***Charles III*** of Spain
(1716-1788), who moreover was friendly to the ideas of the
Enlightenment, and expelled the Jesuits from his dominions.
This in turn destroyed the Paraguay *Reducciones*, crippled
missionary activity in many parts of the empire, and helped
weaken Spanish rule. But by the same token, Charles III in

1760 consecrated all his territories to Our Lady of the Immaculate Conception, and made all public officials swear an oath to uphold that doctrine. Such were the concerns of even the most worldly of Spanish monarchs in those days; well did they earn the hereditary title Alexander VI granted Ferdinand after the taking of Granada: "Most Catholic Majesty."

FRANCE COMES TO AMERICA

France also had a very turbulent history before she was able to send colonists to America. When America was discovered, France was a typical medieval kingdom. In the glorious days of the 13th century, with St. Louis IX she had boasted of one of the greatest kings in Christendom. In France, there developed the *religion royale*, centering around the Holy Ampulla containing chrism delivered by the Holy Ghost to St. Remigius in 496 at King Clovis' baptism at Rheims, and used at the French coronations; the ability of the kings of France to heal scrofula; devotion to the Sacred Heart and the Assumption; and the quasi-priestly characteristics of the French crown, such as receiving communion in both kinds, being members of certain chapters of canons, and being allowed to touch the sacred vessels. France gloried in her title of "Eldest Daughter of the Church" (so called because the Franks under Clovis were the first of the post-Roman Western nations to convert) and in the fact that her kings were, like the Holy Roman emperors, successors to Charlemagne. Dom Guéranger tells us:

> In the baptistery of Saint Mary's at Rheims, the Frank-
> ish nation was born to God; as heretofore on the banks
> of Jordan, the dove was again seen over the waters, hon-
> oring this time, not the Baptism of Jesus, but that of the
> Church's eldest daughter; it brought a gift from heaven,

the holy vial containing the chrism which was to anoint the French kings in future ages into "the most worthy of all the kings of the earth." (*Op. cit.*, vol. XIV, pp.308-309).

But the fair land of France had suffered much in the years after St. Louis. From 1339 to 1453, the Hundred Years War raged in France, as the English kings attempted to secure the French crown (to which they did have some claim). Although at first defeated, the French rallied under St. Joan of Arc in 1429, and began the long process of freeing the lands the English occupied. By 1453, this goal was accomplished. But the country was much weakened. Nevertheless, in 1462, Pope Paul II awarded the monarchs of France the title, "Most Christian king."

Attempts at Settlement

From about 1504, French fishermen sought their livelihood off the Grand Banks of Newfoundland. Twenty years later, King *Francis I* (1494-1547) commissioned *Giovanni de Verrazzano* (1485-1528) to find a Northwest Passage through the Americas to Asia. He reached what is now North Carolina, and proceeded northward. Reaching New York Harbor, he was the first European to gaze on it (which is why the Verrazzano Narrows were given his name much later). He named it the Bay of Saint Margaret. After this he sailed into Narragansett Bay, and met the Wampanoag Indians whom the Pilgrims would be befriended by a century later. His fleet sailed next along the Maine coast, encountered the Abnaki Indians; up to Newfoundland, and then back to France. But he had claimed none of this territory for France. Another ten years would pass before Francis saw fit to try again.

This time, he dispatched *Jacques Cartier* to the New World. Cartier's 1534 voyage led him to the west coast of

Newfoundland, Prince Edward Island, and Anticosti Island. The next year he returned to discover both the Bay and River of St. Lawrence, the latter of which he sailed up as far as the Iroquois village of Hochelaga (present day Montreal). His next voyage was in 1540, whereon he built a fort. Two years later he was joined by the *Sieur de Roberval*. As the Spanish at the same time sought the gold-laden city of Quivira, so too did the French search the St. Lawrence for the wealth-laden Kingdom of Sanguenay, with whose riches Francis hoped to fight Charles V, lord of the Mexican and Peruvian wealth. But try as Roberval might, there was no sign of such a place. Preceded by Cartier, he returned to France in 1543.

Having European wars to worry about, Francis did not bother to send anyone else to the cold and forbidding river valley Cartier had claimed for France. Dying in 1547, he was succeeded by his son Henry II, who was not interested either. In any case, Henry II had problems closer to home. The Protestant Revolt, which had shorn off Northern Europe from the Faith, was threatening France from within. Many nobles and merchants joined the new religion, hoping to benefit from the theft of Church properties, as their counterparts had elsewhere. This resulted in secret plottings just below the surface of French public life. When Henry died in a tournament, his 16-year-old son, Francis II, came to the throne, and the plots quite literally thickened. He died the next year, and his young bride, the beautiful and tragic Mary Queen of Scots returned to her homeland to face the Protestants there–who would in the end engineer her judicial murder.

But in France, Francis' 10-year-old brother, Charles IX, became king with their mother, Catherine de Medici, as regent. Two years later, civil war broke out with the Huguenots (as French Protestants were called). Lasting until 1589, it was a bloody affair of shifting allegiances and atrocities breeding atrocities. The Huguenots took a particular joy in defiling Catholic shrines and sanctuaries, desecrating the Blessed Sacrament and relics of the saints whenever they could. When the war was over, France was again devastated, the last of Catherine's children, Henry III, (and the Valois dynasty) was dead, and the leader of the Protestant faction, Henry IV, converted to Catholicism. He was, after all, the closest heir to the throne.

Success at Last

Unlike his more immediate predecessors, Henry IV had the leisure to consider the lands Cartier had claimed for France more carefully. There was no gold there, but certainly there were furs and perhaps other useful things. More than this, there were souls to be saved, and brought into that Church which the king himself was a new member of. Near at hand was his remarkable Geographer-Royal, *Samuel de Champlain* (1567-1635). His father was a mariner, who took him on a number of voyages. When he was 20, he joined the Catholic Army against the Huguenots. The war ended, he returned to his father's trade, of which he said:

> Navigation has always seemed to me to occupy the first place. By this art we obtain a knowledge of different countries, regions, and realms. By it we attract and bring to our own land all kinds of riches; by it the idolatry of paganism is overthrown, and Christianity proclaimed throughout all the regions of the earth. This is the art...which led me to explore the coasts of a portion of America, especially those of New France, where I have always desired to see the lily [symbol of France] flourish, together with the only religion, Catholic, Apostolic, and Roman. (*Les Voyages du Sieur de Champlain*, Paris, 1613, Pt. V).

After serving in 1598 with the Spanish navy against English pirates off Puerto Rico, he was appointed Geographer Royal to Henry IV in 1601. Two years later, he visited Canada as second-in-command of an expedition which failed to establish a settlement. After more exploratory visits, he founded the city of Quebec on July 8, 1608. What Mexico City, capital of the Viceroy, was to New Spain, so Quebec would be to New France.

But where the Spanish authorities could build on the semi-civilized foundation left by the Aztecs, Incas, and Mayas, and use it as a base for improvement and expansion into less settled areas, the French could not do with the St. Lawrence valley. Its native inhabitants, the Huron and Algonquin Indians, while friendly enough, were primitive hunters with the limited agriculture described in the Introduction. Whatever there would be of civilization in New France, the French would either have to import or make on the spot.

Champlain, however, became as intrepid an explorer of inland rivers as he was of the high seas, venturing down into the present United States. While camped near Ticonderoga, on the lake which bears his name, he joined the Algonquins in a fight against their sworn enemies, the Iroquois. This skirmish in 1609 involved the French in a struggle that would bedevil them for the rest of their North American career.

The Five Nations of the Iroquois (Mohawk, Cayuga, Oneida, Onondaga, and Seneca) were a confederacy of five tribes centered in upstate New York. They were better organized than the surrounding tribes, and were brave and ruthless warriors, delighting in torturing their captives (a habit also known by their neighbors, however). The allying of the French with their Huron and Algonquin enemies resulted in their eventually siding with first the Dutch and then the English against them. It was a great advantage, for the Five Nations were the most effective war-machine in North America. Nevertheless, the French missionaries would make converts among the Mohawk.

Although Henry IV had been assassinated in 1610, his son, Louis XIII did not come of age until 1617. The king faced opposition from some of the great nobles of the realm, from the Huguenots (who had certain fortified cities in their keeping, as given them by the Edict of Nantes, which ended the religious wars), and Germany was about to break out into the Thirty Years War, which pitted the Emperor and the Catholic princes of Germany against the Protestant princes. He could not give New France the attention it required.

The Church, however, was able to provide some help. Four Franciscan Recollects arrived in 1614. In 1625-26, eight Jesuits came to New France, and two years later, 400 settlers. After an English pirate seized the town in 1629, the colony was in their hands for three years, during which time Champlain was a prisoner. But he returned in triumph to the town he had founded, and served as governor until his death.

NEW FRANCE MADE PERMANENT

Once safely back in French hands, the colony was able to begin real growth. Louis XIII was able to take a real interest in New France's growth, as did his chief minister, *Cardinal Richelieu,* who invested heavily. The king, on the other hand, having taken the rebellious Huguenot city of La Rochelle, was as concerned with the spiritual health of his realm on either side of the Atlantic. In 1638, he consecrated his lands to Our Lady of the Assumption:

> We command the Archbishop of Paris to make a commemoration every year, on the Feast of the Assumption, of this decree at the High Mass in his cathedral; and after Vespers on the said day, let there be a procession in the said church, at which the royal associations and the

corporation shall assist, with the same ceremonies as in the most solemn processions.

We wish the same to be done also in all churches, whether parochial or monastic, in the said town and its suburbs, and in all the towns, hamlets, and villages of the said diocese of Paris. Moreover we exhort and command all the archbishops and bishops of our kingdom to have Mass celebrated in their cathedrals and in all churches in their dioceses; and we wish the Parliaments [Provincial high courts] and other royal associations and the principal municipal officers to be present at the ceremony. We exhort the said archbishops and bishops to admonish all our people to have a special devotion to the Holy Virgin, and on this day to implore her protection, so that our Kingdom may be guarded by so powerful a patroness from all attacks of its enemies, and may enjoy good and lasting peace; and that God may so well be served and honored therein, that both we and our subjects may be enabled happily to attain the end for which we were created; for such is our pleasure!

But the king wished to do more for the Faith in a practical way. Eight years earlier, he had given his patronage to a remarkable group called the Company of the Blessed Sacrament. Among its members were *St. Vincent de Paul, Ven. Alain de Solminihac, Bishop Bossuet,* and *Jean-Jacques Olier*, founder of the Sulpicians, as well as many of the greatest names in the realm. The association worked to correct abuses among the clergy, and to help prisoners and the poor. It was responsible for the founding of the General Hospital of Paris and the Seminary of Foreign Missions. Its members worked, moreover, to prevent the then rampant oppression of Catholics by Huguenots in the districts and towns allotted the latter by the Edict of Nantes. They wished also to promote the Faith in New France.

To this end they appointed the 30-year-old *Sieur de Maisonneuve* as governor of a new town, at which he and his settlers arrived in 1642: Montreal. Pious and courageous, he regarded the enterprise as a crusade. From Montreal, missionaries would go out to all the surrounding tribes, including even the Mohawk; that very year, they killed the Jesuit lay brother, *St. Rene Goupil.*

The next year, Louis XIII died, and was succeeded by his five-year-old son, *Louis XIV.* Over the next decade, the saints killed by the Mohawk, the North American Martyrs, included: Ss. Isaac Jogues and John Lalande in New York State, 1646; *St. Antoine Daniel* in Canada, 1648; and *Ss. Jean de Brebeuf, Charles Garnier, Noel Chabanel,* and *Gabriel Lalemant,* all in the Huron country in 1649. These latter, missionaries among the Huron, were all captured when the people they worked amongst were decimated by the Iroquois, who then subjected them to fiendish tortures. Yet their work did produce such fruit as *Bl. Kateri Tekakwitha,* the "Lily of the Mohawks."

Life in New France

But neither the French nor the Hurons were destroyed. They continued a long guerrilla warfare against the Iroquois, which made the French settlers outside the towns very hardy indeed, completing the process begun by the weather. In the towns, particularly in Quebec, an approximation of European culture was kept up, with the governor presiding over a splendid court, and after 1659, a bishop and cathedral.

From 1663 on, New France's administration was regularized. There was in Quebec a Governor-General, similar to the Spanish Viceroys. Under him in Acadia, Montreal, and Trois Rivieres were local Governors, again like the Spanish Captains-General. Assisting him in Quebec was an *Intendant,* responsible for finance, justice, and civil administration. The third important official at Quebec was the Bishop. These three were assisted by a Council, similar again to the Spanish Audencia.

Outside the towns, along the banks of the St. Lawrence, the settlers or *habitants* farmed, generally under a *seigneur*, who, in return for six days of labor a year and nominal rent, directed their defense. During harvest and planting seasons, they worked unremittingly. But in the winter and major feast days, they reveled in Masses, music, dancing, and tale-telling. Under the constant Iroquois threat, they refused to become a somber people, and soon became a match for their Indian enemies at irregular warfare. They would need to be.

Some of the settlers, however, cared little for the towns or farms of New France. Free spirited, they preferred to trap furs with the Indian allies, often taking wives from among them. These were the *Coureurs de bois*, and the *voyageurs*, who used the system of Great Lakes and of rivers, all of which flowed into the St. Lawrence, as their highways into the interior.

With them often traveled Jesuit and other missionaries, the former often encouraged to come to New France by reading of mission exploits in the famed Jesuit *Relations*. These established missions among the tribes contacted by their lay *voyageur* colleagues. Often the fort and the mission were close together; the first to trade furs, the second to evangelize.

Under the influence of such missionaries, many tribes adopted the Faith: the Hurons, the Abnaki, the Algonquins, the Illinois, the Ottawa, and countless others. As the Indians of Florida, New Mexico, and elsewhere provided the Spanish settlements in what is now the United States with support and protection, so too did those who encountered the French. Direct allies of the king, they were essential to the continuance of New France, combining the teachings of Catholicism with whatever of their lifestyle was reconcilable with it.

The Founding of Louisiana

In 1672, the most remarkable of New France's governors was appointed: *Frontenac.* Wishing to challenge English expansionism in North America, he began the construction of a chain of forts along the great lakes. When, in 1677, *Fr. Marquette* and the *voyageur, Joliet,* discovered the Mississippi, the governor was anxious to take advantage of it. The next year, *Robert, Chevalier de La Salle* began his explorations. Reaching the Mississippi himself in 1682, he descended it to its mouth, crossing at some point over the grave of De Soto. He was the first European to reach the Delta.

From 1689 to 1697, France and Britain were at war. When hostilities ceased, the importance of settling the Mississippi valley became obvious. The brothers *Iberville* and *Bienville* set about doing so; by 1712, the towns of New Orleans, Nachitoches, Biloxi, Mobile, Kaskaskia, Cahokia, and Vincennes had been founded. More would follow.

But where New France was cold, Lower Louisiana was tropical, having more in common with the West Indies (where by this time Haiti, Martinique, and Guadeloupe were all French possessions) than Quebec. Instead of furs, sugar became the cash crop. Just as in the West Indies, however, plantation crops meant plantation labor–slavery. As in Spanish territory, slavery was ameliorated by the Church. The *Code Noir* which governed the institution among the French was similar to the Spanish legislation we examined earlier. The result was not only retention of family life among the Blacks, but the rise of a mixed class of Free Men of Color–*gens de couleur libre.* These often retained their French fathers' surnames, inherited property from them (including slaves) and enjoyed French educations.

New Orleans soon rivaled Quebec as a center of culture.

It became world renowned in time, and despite the changes of flags it would suffer, as "the city that care forgot." This name survives today, and serves as a reminder of the gallant Frenchmen who attempted to reproduce the ways of Versailles in a swampy wilderness.

The Fall of New France

The War of the Grand Alliance, as the 1689-1697 War was called (King William's War, to the English colonists), was not the last of the conflicts between France and Spain. Fought as it was in Europe, America, Asia, and the High Seas, it has the dubious distinction of being the first actual world-wide war. It was followed by the War of Spanish Succession (Queen Anne's War) 1701-1713; the War of Austrian Succession (King George's War) 1740-1748; and the Seven Years War (French and Indian War) 1756-1763. These too were all world wars, in the case of the Americas pitting French and Spanish colonies against English. On the side of the French, in particular, were all the affected Indian tribes save two: the Iroquois and the Cherokee. The French had the experience of being continually at war with the Iroquois, and of being conscious of their mission as bearers of the Faith in North America. But the English colonists, although their militias were no match for the French, had a much greater population (since, conditions in Great Britain being rather unpleasant at the time, many English, Scots, and Irish, as well as Germans, were all too eager to come to the New World) and much more military and monetary support from the mother country. The result was that by 1763, all the French possessions east of the Mississippi had fallen to the British (as we must call them after 1707); those west of that river and in lower Louisiana were given to King Louis XV's Spanish cousin, Charles III, to safeguard their inhabitants' religion.

FRENCH AND SPANISH EFFORTS EVALUATED

Although there were many differences between the two nations' policies, and although they sometimes came into conflict in the New World, on the whole the similarities are striking.

Under both powers, there was the same emphasis on correct and impartial administration; education, particularly higher, and the arts; and on public and private works of charity. Similarly, there was the same concern for the spiritual and temporal welfare of Indians and Blacks, to a degree simply unheard of in the English colonies.

Further, there was a certain similarity in the men who guarded and extended the frontiers against hostile Indians and Europeans alike. Among the Spanish, they were the *Soldados de Cuerro*, the "Leather-Jacket Soldiers," superb cavalrymen who with their lances and broad-brimmed hats kept Apaches and Commanches at bay through the trackless desert and mountain wastes of the "Northern Rim of Christendom." For the French, they were the *Coureurs de bois,* the "Runners of the Woods," who were fine boatmen, ever expanding Christendom along the great rivers of North America. The exploits of both groups remind one of the medieval crusaders, just as much as those of the first Conquistadores and navigators do. The reason is simple: the Faith always calls forth the same kind of soldiers for her defense.

Alike also was the official dedication of French and Spanish administration in the New World to the public observance and spread among the Indians of the Catholic Faith. Bishops were important figures, monks, friars and nuns assisted in their work with public funds. The result in both New France and New Spain was a society eminently civilized and eminently humane. That there were lapses, even atrocities, is unquestionable. But these were not the norm, and were generally denounced by the people themselves. These words of Leo XIII in regard to medieval Christendom are almost as applicable to its continuations in the New World:

> There was once a time when States were governed by the philosophy of the Gospel. Then it was that the power and divine virtue of Christian wisdom had diffused itself throughout the laws, institutions, and morals of the people, permeating all ranks and relations of civil society. Then too, the religion instituted by Jesus Christ, established firmly in befitting dignity, flourished everywhere, by the favor of princes and the legitimate protection of magistrates; and Church and State were happily united in concord and friendly interchange of good offices. The State, constituted in this wise, bore fruits important beyond all expectation, whose remembrance is still, and always will be, in renown, witnessed to as they are by countless proofs which can never be blotted out or ever obscured by any craft of any enemies. (*Immortale Dei*, cap. 21).

Where the colonizers fell short of this vision, it was due to the already powerful spirit of secularism, unleashed ultimately by the Protestant Revolt. But by and large, the desire of Queen Isabel and subsequent rulers of Spain and France to erect another part of Christendom on the other side of the Atlantic was fulfilled. What great accomplishments would have resulted had this vision endured is anyone's guess.

In the next chapter, we shall see how that dream was frustrated, and what was built on its ruins.

See APPENDIX I on p. 123 for a list of Spanish and French Royal Remains in North America

THE FOUNDING
OF PROTESTANT
AMERICA
1607-1770

ENGLAND DURING THE PERIOD

The Catholic England of Henry VII, for which Cabot had claimed part of North America, was destroyed by the next king, *Henry VIII*. His declaring himself head of the Church of England began a long series of civil wars and rebellions in England, which would not finally end until 1746 (first of these was the 1536 *Pilgrimage of Grace*, when many North English Catholics, led by *Robert Aske,* demanded restoration of the monasteries; they were betrayed and slaughtered). By the time this occurred, England was both a Protestant nation and mistress of Scotland, Ireland, and an empire which spanned the globe.

Henry, although wanting both rule of the Church in his realm and money from seizure of abbeys and the like, was not in doctrine a Protestant. His Archbishop of Canterbury, Thomas Cranmer, was. After Henry's death in 1547, he was succeeded by his ten year old son, *Edward VI*. During this reign, Cranmer determined religious policy. In 1549, Cranmer introduced an English liturgy to replace the Mass, called *The Book of Common Prayer*. The Catholics of Cornwall and Devonshire rebelled in the *Rising in the West*. This too was defeated. But some Protestants were more radical than others; where Cranmer wanted to retain some prayers, ceremonies, vestments, and so on from Catholic worship, dissenting Protestants wanted to get rid of all of it, and even of bishops (which Cranmer, being one himself, obviously wanted to retain).

When Edward died in 1553, his successor was his older sister, *Mary I*, daughter of Henry's rightful wife, Catherine of Aragon. The next year Queen Mary married *Philip II* of Spain, whom we met in the last chapter. Together, they returned England to the Catholic fold. But their marriage was childless. Henry VIII had had one other daughter, however, by another of his "wives": *Elizabeth I*. In return for her promise to uphold Catholicism in England, she was recognized as heiress by both Mary and the Pope. When Mary died in 1558, she thought that England's return to the Faith was secure.

In this, she was wrong. Elizabeth immediately disavowed her promises, and returned to her father's policies. But England was not the religiously united country Henry had ruled. There were determined Catholics, *Puritans* (who wished to "purify" the Church of all Catholic influence), and all sorts of shades between. So Elizabeth attempted to revive the Church of England in such a way as to make it a compromise between Catholicism and Protestantism, based upon the three pillars of the episcopate, the royal supremacy, and the *Book of Common Prayer*. These things being accepted, one was free to believe what one wished. Since loyal Catholics could not accept these last two, they were subject to intense persecution, and many were martyred both in England

and in Ireland. Her hatred of the Faith was mirrored in her foreign policy: she supported rebels in the Netherlands against Spain, whose shipping she encouraged English pirates to attack; she did her best to subvert the government of her Catholic cousin and heiress, *Mary Queen of Scots.* When Mary was driven into exile in England, Elizabeth imprisoned her. A year later, the 1569 *Rising in the North* saw English Catholics rise in favor of the Scottish Queen, who, Elizabeth having broken her promises, was the rightful Queen of England as well. In 1587, Elizabeth had her executed. To punish his former sister-in-law for this unheard-of action, Philip II attempted an invasion of England with a fleet called the *Armada*. Battered by storms, the Armada was defeated by *Sir Francis Drake* in July 1588.

This last shattered Spanish naval supremacy, and made possible the establishment of English colonies in the New World. Just a year before, *Sir Walter Raleigh* dispatched 117 colonists to Roanoke Island in what is now North Carolina. There was born Virginia Dare, first English-speaking native of the New World. Apparently, a number of these first settlers were refugee Catholics, and young Miss Dare may even have been born to and baptized by Catholic parents. Whatever the case, this was the famous "lost colony"; when a ship reached them the next year, all settlers had vanished without a trace. Only the word "Croatan," carved on a tree in the abandoned village, appeared to give some hint of their fate. Certainly, the Croatoan Indians of today claim to descend from the colony, and bear many of their family names–including Dare. The whole area north of the Spanish territories was named Virginia, after the "Virgin Queen," the unmarried Elizabeth.

The Stuarts

Nevertheless, it was only under *James I* (1603-1625),

Protestant son of the murdered Mary of Scots, that English
settlement in the New World began in earnest. James was a
scholar, and commissioned the Protestant translation of the
Scriptures called the *King James Bible.* But despite his com-
mitment to Anglicanism, his wife, Anne of Denmark, was a
Catholic (although he allowed her co-religionists to be persecuted from time to time). For this and other reasons, the
Puritans began to agitate against the Church of England,
demanding among other things the abolition of bishops.
James opposed this for both political and religious reasons,
holding that both crown and miter came from God ("no
bishop, no king"). A the same time, the Puritans as we shall
see began their migration to the New World, even as they
gathered strength in England.

It was left to James' son, *Charles I,* to oppose them. Since
allied with the Puritans politically were many of the wealthi-
est merchants and landholders in the country who had control of Parliament, religious, political, and economic opposition to the remnants of the Catholic social order in England
coalesced against the king. He too married a Catholic Queen,
Henrietta Maria of France. Allied with him were Catholics,
High-Church (that is, more Catholic minded, as opposed to
Low-Church, more Protestant inclined) Anglicans, peasants,
and much of the gentry and nobility of the more remote
Northern and Western parts of England; similarly, he had
the allegiance of the Highland Scots and Catholic Irish. These
two factions, Parliamentarians and Royalists (called also
Roundheads and *Cavaliers*) first intrigued against each other,
and then fought an open conflict, the *English Civil War.*
Lasting from 1642 to 1646, it resulted in the defeat of King
Charles; in 1649 the triumphant Parliamentarians had him
beheaded. England was ruled by a Puritan dictatorship much
like that in Massachusetts, headed by *Oliver Cromwell.*
Christmas was abolished in accordance with Puritan beliefs,

and mince pies outlawed.

From 1649 to 1660 this state of affairs continued. But after Cromwell's death in 1658, his son Richard was unable to maintain order for more than a year. By popular acclamation, the son of the martyred king, *Charles II*, assumed the throne. Although the Puritans were no longer part of it, the remainder of the oligarchy which had deposed Charles I remained in place, even though on the surface it appeared that the old government had been restored. "The Merry Monarch," as Charles II was known, did not attempt to push the oligarchy, but preferred to operate in non-controversial areas, if possible. He too married a Catholic, the Portuguese princess, Catherine of Braganza. Although Catholics were persecuted at various times during his reign, Charles converted on his deathbed in 1685.

His brother, *James II*, had already done so, although his daughters, *Mary* and *Anne* were raised Protestant beforehand. Because Catholics were by this time a minority in England, James legalized toleration for all Christians, and attempted to strengthen the position of Catholicism in England by appointing many Catholics to high office (the same way in which Anglicanism had become so powerful at the hands of his ancestors). He also tried to rule as a traditional king. This was tolerated by the oligarchy as long as James's heiresses were Protestant princesses who would be amenable to control. But when in 1688 James's Catholic Queen, Mary of Modena, gave birth to a son, they knew that James must be deposed if they were to keep power. The result was the so-called *Glorious Revolution*. The King was deposed, and in his place were brought over from Holland his daughter Mary and her husband *William of Orange*. They became known as William III and Mary II. James' supporters were known as *Jacobites* (from the Latin for James–*Jacobus*). The Scottish Jacobites were defeated in 1689, and the Irish in 1690. William and Mary, and through them the *Whig* oligarchy, now ruled the three Kingdoms.

Under William and Mary (until she died in 1694, after which William ruled alone), Parliament (or rather, those who controlled it) really governed the country. They passed a law in 1689 settling the succession, and declaring that Catholics were ineligible for the English throne. Political power largely gone, William gave away the Crown's financial power to the Whig oligarchs who founded the *Bank of England* in 1694. James II died in exile in France in 1701, and his son, *James Edward*, was proclaimed James III by the Jacobites.

Upon William's death the next year, his sister-in-law Anne became Queen. In 1707, the Parliaments of England and Scotland were merged, and the countries renamed "Great Britain." Taking advantage of the dislike of the Scots for this last measure, James III attempted to land in Scotland in 1708, but his fleet was driven off by a storm. From 1701 to 1713, Britain was involved in a war against France, the *War of Spanish Succession*. The year after it ended, Queen Anne died, having left most of the business of government in the hands of her ministers, who in turn were responsible to Parliament, itself controlled by various factions among the oligarchy.

The Hanoverians

Had her half-brother, James III, been willing to renounce Catholicism, he would have ascended the throne at her death. As he was not, it went to the next closest Protestant relative, the Elector of Hanover, who became King as *George I*. Less than a year after his accession, the Scots Jacobites rose against him, and James III came over to lead them. But although there were pitched battles in Scotland and the North of England, the 1715 rising failed. James went back to France, and George settled down to routine. He spoke no English, and so left practically all matters in the hands of his ministers–preferring to spend time in Hanover, where at least he could speak the language. He died in 1727.

His son, *George II*, was at once better in English (although he did have a thick German accent), and rather more interested in his kingdoms generally. From 1740-1748, Britain was involved in the *War of Austrian Succession,* another world wide conflict. During its course, Prince *Charles Edward*, "Bonnie Prince Charlie," son of James III, led the last Jacobite attempt at regaining the throne for the Catholic Stuarts. Although they invaded England (and George II was actually packing) Prince Charles's lieutenants forced him to retreat into Scotland where they were crushed at Culloden in 1746, a year after the adventure had begun. Although George II tended to clash with his ministers in small things, for the most part he followed his father's lead.

At his death in 1760, his grandson became *George III.* Although the reign started in the midst of the *Seven Years' War* (begun in 1755), it ended triumphantly for Britain three years after the Third George ascended. From the beginning, this King showed a determination to be a true King, as had Charles I and James II. George exerted a certain amount of pressure upon his ministers; in 1765 they came up with the *Stamp Act* to help pay both for the huge debts incurred in defending the American colonies in the last war, and also for their continuing military protection. The next year, James III died, leaving Prince Charles to be hailed as Charles III by the dwindling number of Jacobites; much disappointed in his defeat of two decades earlier, Charles posed little threat to George. Through skillful politicking, George was eventually able to acquire a majority of friendly seats in the House of Commons. Thus, in 1770 he could appoint Lord North as Prime Minister–responsible to himself and not the Oligarchs. So began the era of the King's "personal rule."

FOUNDATION AND GROWTH
OF THE ENGLISH COLONIES

While all this happened in the mother country, colonies were founded, and grew steadily. The first successful settlement was commenced north of the failed Roanoke Colony, at Jamestown in 1607. It was begun at the instigation of the Virginia Company, a joint-stock business formed for the express purpose of settling and exploiting the supposed riches of the land. The first 100 colonists consisted primarily of gentlemen and criminals; workers were few, the more so since the colonists preferred hunting for gold to planting crops. The result was that the first few years were filled with poverty and starvation. Two years after Jamestown was settled, *Lord De La Warr* was appointed Governor of Virginia by King James. He encouraged the growth of the colony and the development of agriculture. By the time of his death in 1618, there were 600 colonists. But it was also during his reign that contact was made with the Powhatan Indians of Virginia, a confederacy of many tribes similar to the Iroquois.

John Smith, an English soldier assigned to help protect Jamestown, was taken prisoner by the Powhatans. His life was saved, however, by the chief's daughter, *Pocahantas*, who put herself between the braves who were going to kill Smith. The chief relented, and Smith was saved. Pocahantas herself later married another Englishman, and died in England. Although there was peace for many years after, increasing settler pressure on them provoked war in 1644. The Powhatans were defeated, and declined steadily; from 8000 in 1607, there were only 2100 in 1669. Today there are about 3000 descendants. Two of the tribes–Pamunkey and Mattapony–retain reservations from the Commonwealth of Virginia, rather than the Federal government.

The year after Lord De La Warr died, the new governor

assembled with his council and representatives of the boroughs or districts which had formed. These representatives became the *House of Burgesses*, and acted as a parliament for the colony. Voting was restricted to property owners. Although Virginia received several other constitutions under the royal government, they were all roughly similar. In 1624 the Company was abolished, and the King appointed a Royal Governor. His council was to be made up of eleven members appointed by the King. The Burgesses would pay the Governor's salary, which made him dependent to a degree on them; he in turn could veto their legislation. Further, the Church of England was the established one in the colony. This meant that Anglican ministers were supported by the colonial government, and that all tax-payers–regardless of their own beliefs–contributed toward it. Just as the King governed the Church of England at home (through his ministers) so too did the Governor in Virginia. Also, all of the laws against Catholics applied in Virginia as well.

These *Penal Laws* restricted Catholics, and were intended to force them to leave the Church and become Protestants. They were very effective: £1 in the money of that time was roughly $50US today. So the penalties were heavy: £100 fine and a month's imprisonment for hearing Mass; fine of £20 a month for not attending Anglican services; high treason to be or to make a convert–punishable by death in various unpleasant ways; high treason to be a Jesuit and felony to shelter one; those convicted of not attending Anglican worship were fined £20 the first month, £40 the next, and £60 the next after that; Catholics were banned from military commissions and public office, nor could they be executors of wills, guardians of children, lawyers, doctors, or pharmacists. Every convicted Catholic was incapable of either defending himself or prosecuting in civil courts, and was fined £100 if found within 10 miles of London–center of court, intellectual, and economic life in England.

Obviously, these laws were not enforced uniformly at all times. Certainly, the Catholics whom the Stuarts took to wife were not bound by them, nor were their friends. In many places, Anglican authorities turned a blind eye to Catholic activities. But the laws were on the books, just as anti-Catholic laws had been in the pagan Roman Empire. Just as then, the laws could be used at any time by local or national officials, for whatever reason. It provoked in the Catholic community continual unease, since they could never know for sure when persecution would start. Many (particularly those with a great deal of money or property to lose) defected as a result.

The Founding of Maryland

Despite the laws against conversion to Catholicism, converts were made. One of these was a good friend of James I and his former secretary of state, *George Calvert, Lord Baltimore*. His son Cecil had already converted. Seeing his coreligionists persecuted so fiercely, he conceived the notion of establishing a New World refuge for them, where they would practice the Faith freely. As a former Protestant himself, however, he wished to give non-Catholics the same freedom in his planned colony. After trying unsuccessfully to establish such a place in Newfoundland's Avalon Peninsula, he turned his sights south. In 1632, on the eve of the granting of a charter to that part of Virginia north of the river Potomac (to be called *Maryland* after both Charles I's Queen, Henrietta Maria, and the Virgin Mary), he died. His son Cecil succeeded to both the title and the dream.

Despite heavy protest by the government of Virginia against the venture, 200 Catholic and Protestant colonists arrived at what is now St. Mary's City aboard the ships Ark and Dove. With them came two Jesuit priests as chaplains, who, after landing, erected a large wooden cross and sang High Mass. We do not know how the Protestant colonists reacted, but we do know that this action was in violation of Lord Baltimore's orders that : "all Acts of the Roman Catholic Religion...be done as privately as may be." However poorly those first Jesuits obeyed this decree, many American Catholics have made it the spirit of their religious practice ever since.

Still, the followers of Lord Baltimore set up a government in conformity with his wishes. Lord Baltimore had complete control, under the King. He had of course an agent in the colony, who had in turn a council and Assembly, in similar fashion to Virginia. Where Maryland differed, however, from her Southern neighbor was that neither the Church of England, not the Catholic Church, nor any other, was established. Rather than subjecting Protestants to the same abuse they themselves had received, they made a great point of granting them equality. As we shall see, it was a tragic blunder.

Life in the Southern Colonies

Maryland and Virginia, and those southern colonies which would be founded later, had no gold nor other profitable minerals. What they did have were fertile soil, plentiful water, and a warm climate. But the very warmth of the climate, and certain other factors, made labor difficult, and small individual plots unprofitable–particularly because tobacco, which grew so well in Virginia and Maryland, and which sold so well in England, requires large scale farming. So developed the *Plantations*; huge farms which were self contained communities, headed by their owners. To work such plantations, however, labor was needed. In the beginning, this was provided by indentured servants, who, in return for having their passage to the New World paid, agreed to work on a plantation or at some other job (depending on their skills). Eventually, criminals and political prisoners (the latter particularly from among the Catholic Irish by Oliver Cromwell) were sent over as virtual slaves. Nevertheless, this was a limited source of essential labor. But in 1619, a Dutch ship landed at Jamestown and sold 20 black slaves from Africa. In time, these would come to dominate the fields of the South.

As we saw in the last chapter, this happened also in the French, Spanish, and Portuguese possessions. Whether we speak of the Plantations of the South and the West Indies, the *Ranchos* of the Southwest, the *Seigneuries* of Canada, the *Haciendas* of Mexico and Central America, the *Latifundias* of Hispanic South America, or the *Fazendas* of Brazil and the *Estancias* of Argentina, we are talking about similar phenomena. Large landholdings in the Americas tend to breed a similar sort of culture. The laborers are generally submissive to authority, hard-working, religious, and carriers of folklore. Often they are black or Indian by blood. The owners usually pride themselves on their family heritage, horsemanship, general culture, and connection to Europe. In much they resemble the feudal lords of Old Europe, of whom Paul Misner writes (*Social Catholicism in Europe,* p.9):

> In an idealized view of this state of things, the squire or lord of the manor was paternally diligent in looking after the arrangements that would assure the prosperity of the little community (or large family). He and his immediate family would plan and supervise the common projects, allow the peasant families enough time and provisions to cultivate their own plots, and settle any problems and quarrels that arose. The peasants in turn would see to it that the soil was properly worked, sown, and harvested with their labor.

Obviously, the ideal and the real are no more often the same in such places than they are anywhere else. But by and large, particularly in earlier times before the Enlightenment, such societies had a level of unity unthinkable to modern people, who think that the terms master and serf, or master and slave, must imply enmity.

Since in the South most non-Catholic Plantation owners were Anglican, they kept up many of the customs of old England, including the great holidays of Christmas and Easter. Money was considered a bad thing to worry about overmuch, and pleasure a good thing. As John Crowe Ransome put it:

> The South never conceded that the whole duty of man was to increase material production, or that the index to the degree of his culture was the volume of his material production. His business seemed to be rather to envelop both his work and his play with a leisure which permitted the activity of intelligence. On this assumption the South pioneered her way to a sufficiently comfortable and rural sort of establishment, considered that an establishment was something stable, and proceeded to enjoy the fruits thereof. The arts of the section, such as they were, were not immensely passionate, creative, and romantic; they were the...social arts of dress, conversation, manners, the table, the hunt, politics, oratory, the pulpit. These were arts of living and not arts of escape; they were also community arts, in which every class of society could participate after its kind. The South took life easy, which is itself a tolerably comprehensive art (Twelve Southerners, *I'll Take My Stand,* "Reconstructed but Unregenerate," p.13).

The Puritans, to whom we must now turn our attention, were quite different.

Puritan New England

In 1620, the *Pilgrims* landed at Plymouth Rock in Massachusetts, arriving on the good ship Mayflower. This was,
in many ways, the real birth of the United States as we know
them. The Pilgrim Fathers are stock-pieces of our national
folklore. We celebrate in emulation of them Thanksgiving
day; our proudest families claim descent from them, and
pride themselves on being Mayflower progeny. The names
of William Bradford, John Alden, Miles Standish, and Priscilla
Mullin are or were (before the decline of education in
America) known to every school-child. But just who were
they?

They were the same sort of Calvinists as the Puritans—
which can be used as a synonym for their beliefs; but where
the Puritans wished to change the Church of England, the
Pilgrims held that she was so Catholic she could not be "Reformed." So, in 1609, 1000 of them settled in Leyden, Holland, where the Calvinist rebels against the Spanish would
be only too happy to have them. But while they were with
their co-religionists, they soon discovered that their children
were becoming Dutch rather than English. After a decade,
they made arrangements with the firm to whom King James
had granted lands north of Virginia, the Plymouth Company. On August 5, 1620, they set off from Southampton.
November 9 found them off Cape Cod, and two days later
they signed the *Mayflower Compact,* an agreement which
bound the signers together into a body for the purpose of
forming a government when they should settle. It was in fact
very similar to the "covenants" members of that religion would
sign when forming a congregation. In late December, they
at last reached Plymouth Rock. Of them, Perry Miller wrote:

> ...[Puritanism's] role in American thought has been
> almost the dominant one, for the descendants of the

Puritans have carried at least some habits of the Puritan mind into a variety of pursuits, have spread across the country, and in many fields of activity have played a leading part....Without some understanding of Puritanism, it may be safely said, there is no understanding of America (Perry Miller and Thomas H. Johnson, eds., *The Puritans*, p.1).

Because of their belief in predestination, and further that predestination to Heaven could be seen by material blessings given by God to His elect in this world, they set great store by wealth. Material success was a sure sign of moral superiority; so everything that contributed to this–thrift, industriousness, and so on, became not merely a means to an end but religious duty. Similarly, those who were poor or enjoyed pleasures other than those of labor were considered damned. Added to this was their hatred of much of the arts; initially because they considered them idolatrous (had they not resulted in Catholic statues and icons?), but finally because they did not in themselves conduce to wealth. To be fair, the Puritans did try to give their tools and implements a certain sparse beauty, but these were legitimate only because they were first and foremost tools, rather than mere ornaments. If a thing or action was pleasant or pleasurable on its own, it was suspect unless also profitable.

Further, identifying themselves with the children of Israel in the Old Testament, they considered all those whom they encountered–Indians, French, Spanish, and even non-Puritan English–to be the equivalent of the Canaanites, and so to be treated the same way, without mercy. Lacking confession, personal sin was elevated from a question for the penitent and his confessor into a matter for the whole community. This in turn encouraged everyone in the settlement to have a much greater interest in the private affairs of their neighbors than would be tolerated in many places. What would have been considered a sin—malicious gossip—in Catholic Europe, became thereby a civic duty.

In much diluted form, these basic attitudes remain very much alive today in this country. In the early days, however, they produced quite an interesting type, as described by Nathaniel Hawthorne in his *The May-Pole of Merry Mount:*

> ...Puritans, most dismal wretches, who said their prayers before daylight, and then wrought in the forest or the cornfield, till evening made it prayer time again. Their weapons were always at hand, to shoot down the straggling savage. When they met in conclave, it was never to keep up the old English mirth, but to hear sermons three hours long, or to proclaim bounties on the heads of wolves or the scalps of Indians. Their festivals were fast-days, and their chief pastime the singing of psalms. Woe to the youth or maiden, who did but dream of a dance! The selectman nodded to the constable; and there sat the reprobate in the stocks; or if he danced, it was round the whipping-post, which might be termed the Puritan May-Pole.

It might also be pointed out, however, that due to the fact that their religion was centered on the Bible alone, the Puritans set great store on reading, and so each village had its school. Self-improvement became a large part of their creed also; with this dual idolatry of the written word and education we see another large part of their legacy.

Although they took eventually to annihilating the Indians, they were at first dependent on their good-will, particularly the first year. Two years later, settlements were made at Portsmouth and Dover, New Hampshire, by similarly minded "godly" folk. But in 1625, *Captain Wollaston* settled at Mount Wollaston or "Merry Mount" as it came to be known. Here was a small settlement and trading-post much more like the English main-stream at the time. As with the French,

Indians were welcome at Merry Mount; whatever was left of Catholic England's culture expressed itself there, and the place stood as both a social and religious alternative to Plymouth. Again, we defer to Hawthorne in the same story just quoted:

> Bright were the days at Merry Mount, when the May-Pole was the banner-staff of that gay colony! They who reared it, should their banner be triumphant, were to pour sunshine over New England's rugged hills, and scatter flower-seeds throughout the soil. Jollity and gloom were contending for an empire.

Alas, gloom triumphed! In 1628, a military column from Plymouth surprised the folk of Merry Mount, and sent most of them back to England. How different would have history been, had the Merry Mounters been as aggressive!

But they were not, and two years after the fall of Merry Mount, another group of Puritans (who retained a nominal connection with the Church of England) arrived and founded Boston. Salem had been founded the same year that Merry Mount fell. On October 19, 1630, the General Court of Massachusetts was convened for the first time, Boston and Salem both being represented. Throughout the following decade, settlers continued to arrive, and the colony of Connecticut was organized. Religious dissenters (including *Roger Williams*, first Baptist minister in the New World) founded Rhode Island as a haven for all Protestant sects and Jews—though not for Catholics. By 1642, Puritan New England, in its basic outline, was formed.

The Dutch in New York and the Swedes on the Delaware

The Dutch Protestant rebels against Spain carried their combat to the high seas. As with the English, Dutch piracy was a prelude to Dutch colonization. Throughout the 17th century they snatched lands from Catholic powers, particularly the Portuguese. In this manner they seized the Spice Islands in the East Indies, Ceylon, Bombay, Malacca, the Gold Coast, and such West Indian Islands as Curacao. To keep open a means of communication with the East, they settled the Cape of Good Hope in South Africa; from these settlers descend the Afrikaaners of today, who retain membership in the Calvinist Dutch Reformed Church and still speak a dialect of Dutch. Early in the century, though, the Dutch dispatched to North America an English sea captain, *Henry Hudson* (d. 1611), who sailed up the river in New York that bears his name in 1609. He failed to discover the Northwest Passage to China which he sought, but he discovered Manhattan Island. In 1613, a trading post was built there, followed the next year by a proper fort; in 1615 one was built at present day Albany, New York. At last, after *Peter Minuit* bought Manhattan in 1626 for $24 (from the Manhattan Indians, who did not own the island anyway), he founded the settlement of Nieuw Amsterdam at the extreme south end of the island. This was the beginning of the great New York City.

To ensure the settlement of the colony, the *Dutch West India Company* which controlled the settlement, granted lands to those men (called *patroons*) who would undertake to settle colonists on them; these were to be quasi-feudal fiefs. The Dutch sold fire-arms to the Iroquois, and in return had little to fear from the Indians, the small tribes in their territories giving little resistance.

Just as the Netherlands became a refuge for Jews and Protestants from Catholic Europe, so too did the New Netherlands. Although the Dutch Reformed Church was established, Portuguese Jews, German and Dutch Lutherans, Protestant Walloons, and many other groups settled in the colony. But then as now, Nieuw Amsterdam had an identity of her own which superimposed itself upon its immigrants.

Although they were Calvinists, the Dutch of New Netherlands practiced their gloomy creed with much less gloom than did their Puritan neighbors to the East. Even the Protestant Revolt could not take every bit of jollity from the Dutch heart; although they hated the Church as much as any good Protestant nation, they retained many of her customs. Not only did they retain Christmas, but as in Holland St. Nicholas continued to visit the children on his feast day, December 6. Indeed, it was through his importation by the Dutch to New York that St. Nicholas survives in this country in the bizarre apparel of Santa Claus. While this last gentleman may certainly be called a cheapened version of the Saint whose mangled name he bears, he is certainly a much more welcome custom than the Puritan non-observance of Christmas, which might have prevailed had the Dutch never come to these shores.

Further, the Dutch of New Amsterdam contributed an important word to American industry: *Baas*, which we call "Boss." The Dutch in New York moreover produced a body of native folk-lore, immortalized by Washington Irving in his "Rip Van Winkle." His *Dietrich Knickerbocker's History of New-York*, while perhaps more amusing than rigorously accurate, nevertheless portrays the Dutch as a pleasing contrast to Hawthorne's Puritans:

> The province of the New Netherlands, destitute of wealth, possessed a sweet tranquillity that wealth could never purchase. There were neither public commotions nor private quarrels; neither parties, nor sects, nor schisms; neither persecutions, nor trials, nor punishments; nor were there counselors, attorneys, catch-poles, or hangmen. Every man attended to what little business he was lucky enough to have, or neglected it if he pleased, without asking the opinion of his neighbor. In those days nobody meddled with concerns beyond his comprehen-

sion, nor thrust his nose into other people's affairs; nor neglected to correct his own conduct, and reform his own character, in his zeal to pull to pieces the character of others... (*op. cit.*, pp.119-120).

Although obviously colored by romanticism, the passage does show what the Dutch in New Amsterdam prided themselves upon. Their stone houses were beautiful imitations of the ones they had left behind in the Netherlands, even down to the colorful tiles around the fireplace; these were often illustrated with scenes from the Bible which allowed the lady of the house to instruct her offspring.

Within four years from the founding of Nieuw Amsterdam, however, conflict arose with the colony's Puritan neighbors. The Dutch had established posts on the Connecticut river. But the colonizing efforts of the Puritans slipped past them in order to found the settlements which became the colony of Connecticut. Rather than fight over the land, the Dutch West India company conceded it to the Puritans in 1638.

In the same year, pressure began to be felt in the South, at the mouth of the Delaware river–land already claimed by Lord Baltimore for his Maryland colony, although not as yet settled by his people. This important area was settled by Swedish colonists, who called their new territory New Sweden. Their first settlement, Ft. Christina (at present day Wilmington, Delaware) was named after Sweden's Queen, who later abdicated to become a Catholic, ending her days in Rome (her tomb is in St. Peter's). The Finns who accompanied the Swedes introduced the kind of house they lived in Swedish-ruled Finland: log cabins. So well adapted to the timber-rich American frontier were they that in time the log cabin became the preferred frontier residence for settlers of all nationalities.

In time, the little Swedish colony became a threat to New

Netherlands; in 1655 the Dutch conquered it, and became masters of a realm stretching from Lord Baltimore's Maryland to the Connecticut Puritans. Such a colony would in normal times be a danger to the English colonial enterprise. But by 1655, the English were deep in other troubles.

THE ERA OF THE CIVIL WARS

As noted in the beginning section, 1642 saw the long simmering conflict between Charles I and his Parliament break out into open conflict. The New England colonies were always in more or less subtle tension with their King, and by their very existence gave moral strength to their co-religionists in England. They declared for Parliament immediately, and then federated as the United Colonies of New England, from which grouping Rhode Island was excluded because of its religious stance. In Maryland, William Claiborne, a Puritan, and Richard Ingle, a pirate, seized control of the government for a year, but were driven out by the populace. Nevertheless, Parliament took control of the colony in 1652, since the proprietor was a Catholic, and imposed the penal laws. The same year witnessed the overthrow of *Sir William Berkeley*, the Royal Governor of Virginia. With this last development, the colonies, like the mother country, were under the sway of Oliver Cromwell, who in turn exported many Irish as slaves to the New World.

The Restoration

Oliver Cromwell died in 1658; his son Richard attempted to continue the Commonwealth. But the next year Sir William Berkeley was restored to power in Virginia, and Charles II proclaimed King, foreshadowing his restoration in England itself in 1660. Maryland quickly returned to the rule of Lord Baltimore as well. But in New England, careful negotiations were required, first to assure royal supremacy in the province, and then to convince the colonies there to accept new charters binding them more closely to the home government (thereby weakening the Puritan establishment). Eventually, agreements were come to; but the Puritans remained quick to seize whatever power they could from the crown.

Meanwhile, New Netherlands continued to grow and prosper, presenting at once a danger to the neighboring colonies and a tempting target. England and the Netherlands being at war, it was resolved that New Netherlands must be taken. They were granted by King Charles to his Catholic brother, James, Duke of York, who had reorganized the Royal Navy after the confusion of Cromwell. He was a good admiral and a skilled soldier.

His opponent was the Dutch governor, *Peter Stuyvesant*. A doughty old soldier, who had lost a leg fighting in South America, he it was who conquered New Sweden. When in August 1664 an English fleet of four ships appeared in the harbor and demanded surrender, Stuyvesant refused, replying in a letter:

> As touching the threats in your conclusion, we have nothing to answer, only that we fear nothing but what God (who is just as merciful) shall lay upon us, all things being in His gracious disposal; and we may as well be preserved by Him with small forces as by a great army; which makes us wish you all happiness and prosperity, and recommend *you* to his protection.
>
> My lords,
> Your thrice humble and affectionate servant and friend,
>
> P. Stuyvesant

Despite the valor of the governor, however, the walls of the little fort were tumbling down, and the Dutch troops were very few. So the populace and the governor's council demanded he surrender. He did so, but was dragged from the walls by the Dutch minister declaring that he would rather be dead.

Still, he stayed in the colony, and died many years later, loved and respected by both English and Dutch; his bones were laid in the church of St. Mark-in-the-Bouwerie, and his descendants too continued for several centuries as one of the first families of the city. Here again, though, as with Merry Mount, one wonders what might have happened had the influence of the jollier Dutch prevailed over that of the Puritans.

After the conquest, the Duke of York found himself in control of the Hudson Valley, present day New Jersey, eastern Pennsylvania, and Delaware. Both colony and its capital were renamed New York in his honor. Confirmations were given to the Patroons of their status, and as Lords of the Manor, the same was given to later arrivals under the same rules. The Duke almost immediately granted New Jersey to two of his friends, however, who named it after the island of Jersey, over which one of them had been governor.

Indians, Spaniards, and rebellion

In 1663, a group of eleven lords were granted the territory south of Virginia stretching to Florida, which they named "Carolina" for the King. After a few false starts, the first settlement, Charleston, was founded in 1670. The new town and its environs, being semi-tropical in environment, lent themselves to such plantation crops as rice and indigo. Many of Charleston's first settlers were as a result planters from Barbados and French Huguenots (after the latter were expelled from France in 1687) who gave the town an aristocratic tone it has never since lost.

But the ever expanding Carolina settlers eventually came into contact with the Northern edge of Spanish Florida. Conflict was certain.

Meanwhile, the New England colonies also continued to expand, with ever more Puritan settlers occupying ever more Indian lands. Already in the 1630's the settlers in Connecticut had destroyed the Pequot tribe. In Massachusetts, the Wampanoags, the Indians with whom the Pilgrims had shared the first Thanksgiving, began to feel the increasing pressure of white expansion. Thus the friendship of chief *Massasoit* turned eventually into enmity on the part of his son, *King Philip*. More and more the Indians were pressured to accept Puritan oversight of their tribes and regulation of hunting and so on. As a defensive measure, he leagued most of the Indians from Maine to Connecticut. But when three Wampanoags were executed for the murder of a spy by Massachusetts authorities, the young braves demanded revenge. War broke out in June 1675.

At first, with the element of surprise, the Indians had the upper hand. White settlements across the New England frontier burned, with men, women, and children dead. The militia retaliated with equally bloody assaults on Indian villages. In December, the Great Swamp Flight in Rhode Island decimated the Narragansetts, Philip's closest allies. Nevertheless, the Indians managed to hold the upper hand until the spring of 1676. The summer was disastrous, and in August, Philip was captured and shot and his young son sold as a slave. Soon Indian resistance was broken—half the Wampanoags were sold into slavery in Bermuda, whence many a Bermudan has Indian features today. Whole villages had been massacred, and many of the remnants fled north to Canada and the French, or else sought refuge with the Mohawk, who had sympathized with the revolt. Those who remained were put on reservations, and most of their lands in southern New England opened for settlement. But more than 600 white men had been killed–over a sixth of the male population of New England. Still, it was a complete triumph for the Puritans.

Even so, there were reverberations elsewhere. Indians further south were agitated as a result, some of the Susquehanna, for instance, going on the warpath on the Maryland frontier. This led to defensive preparations in Virginia. There the governor, the long-serving Sir William Berkeley, attempted a sort of static defense by supporting presumed friendly Indians and monitoring possibly hostile tribes. One of the Burgesses, *Nathaniel Bacon,* urged an aggressive policy against all Indians in Virginia. On 23 June he appeared in front of the statehouse with 500 thugs, their weapons cocked and ready. They demanded that Bacon be given command of the provincial forces for a war against all the Indians in the colony. The assembly capitulated, Jamestown was in Bacon's hands, and Sir William fled across the Chesapeake to the Eastern Shore. Bacon meanwhile set off to attack the Pamunkeys, up to now steady allies of the English. Sir William recaptured Jamestown, which caused Bacon to cut short his plundering mission, and retake the capital, which he burned and evacuated. Dying of natural causes on October 26, he left his disorganized followers to be defeated by the septuagenarian Sir William. When troops arrived from England they found Virginia at peace. Later historians have often considered Bacon's rebellion to have been a rehearsal for the American Revolution.

At the same time, more settlers continued to arrive in Carolina. As they did so, English raids into the Florida province of Guale became more frequent. At last, in 1680, a band of English-allied Creek Indians attacked the northernmost mission, Santiago de Ocone on Jekyll island. A few of the

Indians of the mission were killed, but the remainder under a single Spanish officer held off the attack. Shortly thereafter, Santa Catalina on St. Catherine's Island was assaulted by 300 English-led Indians. One Captain Francisco Fuentes fended them off with five Spanish and sixteen Indian musketeers. Despite these and other such acts of bravery, the Spanish governor at St. Augustine ordered the northernmost missions abandoned.

This was a mistake, because the Indians involved considered retreat cowardice. In 1684, these tribes defected to the English. They then in turn began raiding farther south into Spanish territory themselves. With only 290 Spanish soldiers, the governor in 1686 decided to withdraw troops and missions south of the St. Mary's River, then as now the northern frontier of Florida. But the English were not interested in evangelizing their new allies. Missions they could destroy; they would not replace them.

Penn's Woods

Sir William Penn was another friend of the Duke of York, and a convert to Quakerism. He wished to establish a colony where all men, even Catholics, could worship as they pleased. The Duke, being Catholic, was pleased by the idea of another place in the colonies where his co-religionists might be free, and granted Penn an area to be called "Penn's Woods"– Pennsylvania–in 1681. The next year the settlement of Philadelphia, the city of "Brotherly Love" was founded.

From the beginning, Pennsylvania was a melting pot. In addition to the Quakers, many Ulster Scots settled on the frontier, and closer to Philadelphia were Germans. These latter belonged to many different sects–Lutheran, Mennonite, Amish, German Reformed, and Moravian–as well as the Catholic Church. Calling themselves *Deutsch*, Germans, they were and are called "Pennsylvania Dutch." Their culture survives even today, and the Pennsylvania Dutch country is still a world apart.

Good King James

King Charles II had been much more successful than anyone had supposed he would be. J.M. Sosin observes:

> From almost the onset of the rule of Charles II, men in America, especially the more zealous Puritans in New England, had expected the restored monarchy to collapse. As one year succeeded the next, Charles remained on the throne, although the King and his ministers seemed unable to exert their will on the plantations across the Atlantic....Charles II proved to be a much more adept politician and a more tough-minded ruler than his father. He survived the hysteria raised by the Popish Plot and broke the attempt by the Parliamentary opposition to control the throne by excluding his brother from the succession. During this extended crisis at home, king and ministers could devote little attention to affairs across the Atlantic. By the close of 1682, however, the monarchy seemed in a stronger position as a result of the reaction to the extremist tactics employed by the political opposition in and out of Parliament....Only then did Charles and his ministers attempt to impose some order. But time had almost run out; Charles had but a short time left to his life (*English America and the Restoration Monarchy of Charles II*, p.167).

Indeed, the Merrie Monarch died, a repentant Catholic, in 1685. His brother, the Duke of York, succeeded him as James II. James was the first Catholic to ascend the throne since Queen Mary in 1553. But 132 years had changed much. Mary had ruled over a country still primarily Catholic, which rejoiced in a return to the old religion. James presided over a nation with a large Protestant majority. Further, Mary's opposition had been poorly organized; James's was not, had

had the experience of running the nation already, and possessed also the precedent of having beheaded James's father.

For all this, while James wished to see Catholicism triumphant in England, he was well aware that this would take time, even as weaning Englishmen from the religion of their ancestors had taken time.

The religious question was not the only one which concerned the new king, however. Already he had appointed the Catholic *Thomas Dongan* as governor of his colony of New York before he was king. At that time he realized that the major weakness of the colonies was their disunity. He was resolved to remedy this.

At the time of James's accession, there were over 150,000 settlers scattered from Maine to Carolina. While England and France were at peace, their interests on the northern frontier often collided, and might precipitate conflict at any time. James was concerned that, as things stood neither the New England colonies nor New York could stand a determined assault on their own from Canada. They must be welded into one strong colony, therefore.

The King appointed *Sir Edmund Andros* as governor of New England. Sir Edmund arrived at Boston to take up the reins of Massachusetts government on December 20, 1686. A few days later, he assumed the rule over Rhode Island. On October 18, 1687, he received orders from London to annex Connecticut to the "Dominion of New England," as the new super-colony was to be called. Sir Edmund traveled to Hartford and took control of that colony on November 1. New Hampshire, New York, and New Jersey were also added to the Dominion. It appeared that James's plan would succeed.

But there were several problems brewing. One was that Sir Edmund's review of land titles went against the claims of various wealthy speculators in the Dominion. Another was his insistence that one of Boston's three Puritan churches allow Anglicans to worship there on Sunday morning.

The Un-"Glorious" Revolution

The overthrow of King James II in 1688 undid all the progress in colonial unity he had accomplished. Puritan New England had in any case hated both him and his brother, accepting them only grudgingly. When on 18 April the news of James's overthrow arrived in Boston, a mob including hundreds of militiamen arrived in Boston, disarmed Andros' guard of 15 men, and took them to prison. In each of the other New England colonies, those who had held office prior to the organization of the Dominion ejected Sir Edmund's officials and returned to power.

In New York, a group of rebels led by one *Jacob Leisler*, an apparently paranoiac rabble rouser, took control of the city. But Leisler's rule was confined to Manhattan. There however, anyone might be accused of being a "Papist" and removed from office or employment. Eventually, a governor was appointed from England, the city subdued, and Leisler tried for treason and executed.

In Pennsylvania, the local establishment took advantage of Penn's well-known friendship with James to take over effective rule of the colony, although Penn remained officially in charge. Carolina's and Virginia's governments simply proclaimed William and Mary as King and Queen.

Maryland was, of course, a different case. Like his father and grandfather, the third Lord Baltimore, Charles Calvert, allowed Protestants to freely settle in Maryland and enjoy full civil rights. By 1689, they were a majority of the population. A group of the more wealthy and influential formed, when the news from London arrived, the Protestant Association. On July 27, the Association seized the capital at St. Mary's City. In 1690, King William officially took control of the colony, and voided the rights of the Catholic proprietor. The Assembly made it illegal for Catholics to hold office in Maryland.

THE STRUGGLE AGAINST CATHOLIC AMERICA

The major ally of James II, even in exile, was France's King Louis XIV. He was already engaged in war with the Grand Alliance of the Holy Roman Empire, Spain, Sweden, Bavaria, Saxony, and the Palatinate. When William usurped the throne, he immediately brought England into the conflict, known as "King William's War" in the colonies.

Toward the end of 1689, the Iroquois allies of the English staged the horrible Lachine massacre, against the little town near Montreal. The reaction of the French and their Indian allies was swift and deadly. On February 8, 1690, Schenectady, New York was similarly served by them. Raids hit other frontier villages, but in April of that year, *Sir William Phips* seized the French naval base of Port Royal in Acadia. The war then settled down into skirmishes.

Witchcraft at Salem

While more exposed areas were undergoing attacks by French and Indians, Massachusetts had little to fear from earthly enemies. But the Puritans, still imbued with the gloomiest Calvinism such worthies as *Increase* and *Cotton Mather* could give them, attempted to continue building their "city on a hill." The encounter between the darkest European heresy and the dark and still pagan New England hills must have been a difficult one indeed. Fr. Montague Summers describes the problem well:

> There can be no doubt that the settlers in New England were not only firm believers in every kind of Witch-

craft, but well primed in every malevolent superstition that could commend itself to their verjuiced and tortured minds. They looked for the devil round every corner, and saw Satan's hand in every mishap, in every accident. The Devil, in fact, played a larger part in their theology than God. They were obsessed with hell and damnation; their sky was cloudy and overset; their horizon girded with predestination and the awful consciousness of sin. It is almost impossible to conceive the effect of a new land, a strange mysterious borne beyond the waves of the illimitable Atlantic, must have had upon the muddied morbid minds and tortured souls of these stern and stoic pioneers (*The Geography of Witchcraft*, p.256).

This provided a sort of mental pressure cooker which, from time to time, produced mass hysteria of various sorts. In the case of Salem, it began in the long winter nights of 1691 and 1692, when friends and family of the Reverend Samuel Parris, minister at Salem, would gather to listen to the weird tales of voodoo and magic told by the Parrises' female slave, Tituba. Soon, three of the young girls who had heard the tales declared themselves bewitched, and accused three women of Salem of doing it to them. More and wilder tales were told and fits performed. The number of bewitched grew slowly, that of the accused by leaps and bounds. After conviction, the witches were put to death by "pressing" with rocks or by hanging. Over 20 had been executed by October of 1692. Finally, the Royal Governor, Sir William Phips (the victor of Port Royal) stepped in, and forbade the special courts to hear any more Witchcraft case; further he decreed that the regular courts were no longer to accept spectral evidence. Finally, he ordered all prisoners discharged in May of 1693, and the 200 inmates returned to their homes.

The repercussions of the case have reverberated down to

our own day. On the one hand, the great grandson of Judge
Hathorne, Nathaniel Hawthorne, was haunted by a sense of
familial guilt which inspired much of his best work. Arthur
Miller's play, *The Crucible,* was set during the affair at Salem,
and it is continually invoked in our popular culture. But as
we shall see, it was not the last outbreak of mass hysteria in
our country.

In this same year of 1692, however, as a sort of mourn-
ful counterpoint to the events at Salem, the Assembly of
Maryland forbade Catholics there to act as attorneys.

The Martyrdom of Fr. Plunkett

After five more years of skirmishing, King William's War
finally drew to a close. In that same year, however, there died
in Virginia a martyr for the Catholic Faith, Fr. Christopher
Plunkett, whose story should be better known. He was born
to a noble Irish family in 1649. At 21 he became a Capuchin, and in 1680 he arrived in Virginia, at the estate of his
cousin, John Plunkett. The *Annali Cappucini* tells his story
(III, 540-542):

> Father Christopher undertook his voyage with a vig-
> orous and cheerful spirit. He sailed happily, looking back
> to the shores of his beloved fatherland. Combining great
> prudence and zeal, he went to the enemies of the Catho-
> lic Faith and offered himself a courageous and indefati-
> gable apostle.

Penetrating deeply into the remote villages and inhospi-
table forests, he approached timid Catholics who had been
frightened by the pressure of persecution. He encouraged
them by his eloquent words and instilled in them resigna-
tion and faith in the power and goodness of God. And to
many who had been ensnared by erroneous doctrine he
brought light and explanation, so that he not only strength-
ened the holy faith of the many Catholics who had fallen

into this deception, but even converted heretics and brought them into the bosom of the Catholic Church.

And although he was very careful to avoid the snares of the Protestant princes who ruled the whole island, he fell into their hands and was harshly treated. Relentlessly they dragged him from one to another galley, with beatings and with sufferings of hunger and thirst.

The intrepid Father Christopher bore all with an unconquerable spirit, rejoicing in his heart that he was able to suffer after the example of our Lord Jesus Christ. They not only wanted to weaken his firmness of faith by coaxing and alluring him to do so, but also to have him among the preachers of Calvinism; but in vain, for he was as solid as an immovable bulwark.

Seeing, therefore, that they were not able to defeat and subdue him, they condemned him to exile, confining him to a barbarous island on which there was no one but heretics and enemies of Catholics. In that place the invincible Fr. Christopher saw sorrow, until he ended the captivity of men by passing into the sweet and perpetual liberty of God.

He died alone and abandoned on that brutal island in the forty-eighth year of his age and the twenty-seventh in religion. His death is registered in this year of 1697.

Fr. Plunkett's sufferings were emblematic of what all English-speaking Catholics would have to go through, if in less unpleasant ways. Two years after the sainted Capuchin died, William III decreed even more restrictions for Catholics: 1) Any bishop or priest exercising his office or any Catholic keeping a school to be imprisoned for life; 2) £100 reward for the capture of any priest or the conviction of a Catholic sending his children overseas to be educated; and 3) no Catholic refusing the Oath of Supremacy and the Declaration Repudiating Transubstantiation could buy or inherit land.

The Ruin of Spanish Florida

The War of Spanish Succession having broken out, and Spain being allied with France, the English in Carolina resolved to finish the job begun twenty years earlier. On October 22, 1702, Governor James Moore arrived in front of St. Augustine with a thousand men–half English, half Indian allies. Unable to reduce the fort, the English made their revenge on outlying churches and missions, killing many of the Indians thereat, and taking 500 away as slaves.

Two years later, Moore returned, this time to what is now the Florida Panhandle, then the abode of the Apalachee Indians. He commenced his work there with an assault on a mission and its surrender. Then:

> Word of the attack reached the nearby presidio of San Luis Patali, and Captain Alonso Dias Mexia, with thirty Spaniards, two friars, and four hundred Indians, rushed to give assistance. Twice they drove Moore back, but in the evening they...ran out of ammunition and had to surrender. Moore was immensely satisfied with himself....At Ayubale, and the next day at Patali, his men slew the three priests, and committed acts of gratuitous barbarity on the Christian Indians. Fray Juan de Parga Araujo was beheaded, and his body butchered. Fray Manuel de Mendoza's body was later found in a charred state, his hands and a half-melted crucifix sunk into his flesh. Father Miranda's remains were never found. To a Spanish rescue party that reached the two towns several days later, the scene was one of indescribable horror: scalped and mutilated bodies of men, women, and children lay about the ground, or hung from stakes. The few survivors who came out of the blood-bath to tell the tale had consoling tales of heroism. The governor passed them on to the king: "During this cruel and barbarous martyrdom which the poor Apalache Indians experienced, there were some of them who encouraged the others,

declaring that through martyrdom they would appear before God; and to the pagans they said, "Make more fire so that our hearts may be allowed to suffer for our souls. We go to enjoy God as Christians" (Michael V. Gannon, *The Cross in the Sand,* pp.75-76).

The missions in Florida never recovered from these blows. By 1708 the remaining mission Indians had been gathered within the walls of St. Augustine. In the meantime, ten to twelve thousand Indians had been taken to Carolina as slaves. The beautiful hybrid civilization developed in Florida was completely destroyed.

Well does Dr. Gannon wonder why no "Black Legend" ever grew up around James Moore.

The Rest of the War

1704 saw a political victory for the Protestants in Maryland as great as Moore's in Florida was for Carolina. In that year the Assembly passed the Act to Prevent the Growth of Popery. This prohibited Catholic worship and forbade priests to make converts or to baptize any but children of Catholic parents. The wealthier Catholics of the colony petitioned for a temporary reprieve from the first clause in respect to private homes; in an extraordinary move, Queen Anne intervened to make the exception permanent. Because of this, Catholic Maryland survived. The peculiarly English Catholicism that yet remains in parts of Maryland like St. Mary's and Charles Counties, the Eastern Shore, and the area in the north of the State around Mt. St. Mary's and Emmitsburg, and which was later brought to the "Holy Land" of central Kentucky in such places as Loreto and Holy Cross, owes its survival thereby to Queen Anne.

On other fronts, the French and Spanish tried unsuccessfully to take Charleston in 1706; 1710 did see the successful capture of Port Royal by the English, who renamed it

Annapolis Royal after their Queen. Two years later a revolt by the Tuscaroras of Carolina was put down with great bloodshed, and the survivors fled to the Iroquois, who made them a "Sixth Nation." At last, in 1713, peace was signed; in North America, France ceded Hudson's Bay, Newfoundland, and Nova Scotia to Great Britain, although the French-Acadians who lived in the latter place were allowed to stay.

The Long "Peace"

Although peace had been declared, sporadic raiding by Indians allied with all sides continued. More immigrants continued to arrive from various parts of Europe to the English colonies, and agriculture and trade increased correspondingly. In New England, the Salem Witch trials had badly discredited much of the Calvinist establishment. As Fr. Montague Summers opines: "The Genevan ministers had neither the spiritual nor the practical knowledge to deal with so dark and difficult a task. Naturally they blundered woefully and abundantly. As in England, their mistakes have provided the sceptic and the materialist with many a text for trite moralizing and meditation upon the ignorance of our forefathers" (*op. cit.*, p.348). An element of doubt entered into the New English mind, which, when it encountered new, unbelieving currents of thought, would end by destroying faith in any sort of Christianity at all among many of the more educated former Puritans.

But internal demons aside, New England in the 1720's faced another foe: the Abnaki Indians of northern Maine and today's Maritime Provinces of Canada. The last had been converted to Catholicism by the French Jesuits and were steady allies of the nation who had brought them the true religion. Moreover, they had also supported King Philip, and gave refuge to many of the defeated in that war.

In 1694 there came among the Abnaki of the valley of

the Kennebec a new Jesuit missionary, Fr. Sebastian Râle, S.J. He was a diligent pastor, beloved by his flock, for whom he composed in their own language a catechism, and in the same language translated the common Catholic prayers. Setting up his headquarters at the village of Norridgewock, he stayed with his people throughout King William's War, several times fleeing marauding English bands with them.

When 1713 brought peace, the English agreed to leave the Abnaki in peaceful possession of their lands. But before long the settlers began encroaching upon them again. War broke out in 1721 as a result, and the New Englanders resolved to capture Fr. Râle, whom they considered to be the heart of the resistance. In August of 1724, the English attacked Norridgewock while all the men were out hunting. To give his flock time to escape, he went out to meet the invaders. The old missionary was shot at the foot of the village cross, his body catching a hundred bullets. His body was then mutilated. Fr. Râle's scalp was taken back to Boston and paraded around the streets.

Elsewhere in the colonies, the same pattern of growth in settled areas and skirmishing on the frontiers continued. Northern Carolina had become home to many small farmers and merchants, whereas the southern part of the colony continued to develop along the lines of plantation economy. Strife between the two sections became so intense that at last the government in Britain separated the two areas into the colonies of North and South Carolina in 1729. Due to the highly stratified and aristocratic nature of society in Virginia and South Carolina, North Carolinians took to calling themselves "a valley of humility between two mountains of conceit."

Although Governor Moore and various other worthies of the same sort had devastated Spanish Florida's interior, St. Augustine remained inviolate due to its fortifications. Driven out of the south of Carolina by the English, the Yamasee Indians had sought refuge at St. Augustine with the Spanish. From there they had continued to harass the English, until a raid nearly wiped them out in 1727. But with the land between the Spanish frontier and Charleston being basically empty of all save warlike Indians and brigands, South Carolina was not secure.

An answer appeared in the person of James Oglethorpe, an English philanthropist. In Britain in those days, one could be imprisoned for debt. He would stay in Debtor's Prison until and unless his debts were paid. Naturally, it was rather difficult to earn money while imprisoned, and so for many debtors it was a life sentence, unless friends or relations could or would bail them out. Charles Dickens' father, in a later time, went there; this is why the young Dickens had to work as a child.

Oglethorpe conceived the idea of a refuge for such prisoners in America, where they could start over. The Crown, in the meantime, looked at the empty portions of South Carolina as a security risk, and longed for colonists to settle it. The two ideas were joined, and in 1733 Oglethorpe led the first band of settlers to the new town of Savannah, in the new colony of Georgia, named after King George II. All thirteen colonies were founded, and South Carolina had a buffer against the Spanish. Its effectiveness would shortly be tested.

King George's War

The hatred of Spain which had so long characterized the English was always easily inflamed. In the late 1730's, another wave of anti-Spanish hysteria gripped the British public. During a Parliamentary debate on the topic in 1738, a certain Captain Jenkins appeared, exhibiting what he claimed was his ear, cut off by Spanish coast guards in 1731. Whatever the truth of the affair, it was enough to cause a declaration of war–a conflict called, appropriately enough, the War of Jenkin's Ear.

One year after the war began, James Oglethorpe tried his hand at generalship. With 1200 men he set out to besiege St. Augustine. For 37 days he kept at it. Despite being outnumbered, however, the garrison and populace refused to given in. Whenever the British let loose a cannonade, the besieged Spanish, led by their bishop, Francisco de San Buenaventura y Tejada, would join in a chorus of *Ave Maria!* Discouraged at last, Oglethorpe and his men retreated to Georgia.

Semi-comic as this episode was, the war in general fanned the fanatical anti-Catholic hatred of the colonials. In 1741, New York City was rocked by an affair called the **Negro Plot**, which led to the death of one Fr. John Ury as yet another martyr to American Protestantism. It began due to rumors spread about a rash of unexplained fires. These, it was said, were being set by blacks at the instigation of priests as a prelude to burning the entire city. Panic began to set in. The Lieutenant-Governor, George Clarke, despite having proved that at least one of these fires was certainly an accident, a few weeks later claimed to have discovered a conspiracy to destroy the city. He offered a good deal of cash and a pardon to any white who would come forward with information about the plot. An indentured servant named Mary Burton claimed to have information and took the reward. Based on her evidence, three blacks were hung, although no real proof had been produced that there was any conspiracy at all. An atmosphere prevailed in New York not unlike that at Salem 49 years before.

Clarke then offered an amnesty to any black who would come forward and reveal what he or she knew. Hoping to free themselves from any possible accusation, many did so–

telling wild self-contradictory tales which nevertheless were
enough to cause arrests. At last, Mary Burton surfaced again
with an accusation against one John Ury; both that he was in
on the plot and that he was in fact a Catholic priest (for
which offense alone he could be executed). Ury was arrested
and tried. During his interrogation, although he denied in-
volvement in any plot, he refused to answer whether or not
he was a priest. He was accused of teaching children catechism in a secret school in New York, performing baptisms,
and gathering folk in his room to celebrate Mass. There were
no papers or any proof that he was a priest or even a Catholic,
but his silence was enough to condemn him. There has been
some question as to whether or not he was indeed a Catholic
priest, but the fact that he maintained silence when a single
word could have saved his life seems conclusive; he would
not have admitted it however, in order to protect his secret
flock. Some have suggested that perhaps he was an Anglican
Jacobite who would not take the oath to King George–but
he could have said so and saved himself from hanging. His
last words were published in Philadelphia shortly after, and
only the Catholic network of the time could have done this,
some of their number having witnessed the hanging.

The deaths of the blacks were horrible. Eleven were burnt
at the stake and twenty hanged. Most were raised in the
English or Dutch colonies, without religion, and went to
their deaths screaming in despair. But some had been freed
by the Spanish and died as true Catholics, clutching their
crucifixes. Typical of these is this account from the register
of the day:

> Juan de Sylva, the Spanish Negro condemned for the
> conspiracy, was this day executed according to sentence:
> he was neatly dressed...behaved decently, prayed in Span-
> ish, kissed a crucifix, insisting on his innocence to the
> last.

Thus died a group of Catholics, victims of the same murderous temper against the Faith which from time to time breaks out in all heathen lands.

Back in the South, the Spanish attempted in 1742 to take Savannah with a force of 3000. Just as they had repelled Oglethorpe two years earlier, so he returned the favor now. Exhausted, the two sides settled down to a war of attrition.

Two years later, the War of Austrian Succession broke out, pitting Austria and Great Britain against Prussia, France, Spain, Bavaria, and Saxony. Being yet another world war, it was called King George's War by the British colonists; it absorbed the sputtering War of Jenkin's Ear.

Although the French had ceded Acadia, the mainland of Nova Scotia, to Britain, she retained Cape Breton Island, called Isle Royale. On that island, to make up for the loss of the naval base of Port (called by the English Annapolis) Royal, was built the great town and fortress of Louisbourg, named after King Louis XV. As long as it remained in French hands, there would be possibility of a French fleet sweeping down on Boston. On April 30, 1745, a force of 4000 British troops under *William Pepperell* landed and began to lay siege to Louisbourg. At last, on June 16 the city fell.

The rest of the conflict was marked by false starts and campaigns that never left the planning stage on both sides. Frontier warfare continued with all its horror and atrocity. At last, the belligerents in Europe made peace, and returned all conquests made. Louisbourg was again in French hands.

The End of New France

In the years after the peace accord, the French in Canada built a network of forts in the Ohio country (the present states of Ohio, Indiana, Illinois, Kentucky, West Virginia, and Western Pennsylvania) to secure their claims. In 1753, the Royal Governor of Virginia, which colony claimed those lands, dispatched the youthful colonel *George Washington* to protest the presence of the French in what they considered Virginian land. The French commander sent the protest to the Governor at Quebec. The next year, Washington returned with a body of troops, but was defeated and captured, although allowed to withdraw afterwards–ironically on July 4.

War clouds were stirring elsewhere in the world as well. On the frontier the first shots would be fired in the Seven Years' War. General William Braddock was sent from England to take command in North America. He chaired a convention of the royal governors which decided upon a three pronged strategy requiring assaults on Ft. Duquesne (present day Pittsburgh), Ft. Niagara, and Crown Point.

At that time, a detachment of 3000 Massachusetts militia took the French forts Gaspereau and Beausejour on the Nova Scotia isthmus. That deed done, they turned their attention to the 7000 French-Acadian settlers who had dwelt peacefully under British rule since 1713. These were given the choice of going into exile or renouncing their Catholicism and allegiance to the King of France. They chose exile. From Florida to Maine they were parceled out along the shore, with no regard to separation of families. Eventually, many made their way to the bayous and prairies of Louisiana where they were the ancestors of today's Cajuns. Others returned to France, settling on islands off France's West coast. Many others returned north. Finding their old country occupied by Puritan settlers from New England they settled parts of Cape Breton and the "French Shore" of Southern Nova Scotia. Still others went to Quebec's Magdalene Islands and southern Gaspe Peninsula, to Prince Edward Island, and to New Brunswick. Some of these last penetrated eventually deep into the interior, along the St. John's river valley, which today is the French speaking Madawaska region of Maine. The whole affair was immortalized by Henry Wadsworth Longfellow in his poem *Evangeline*.

At the same time, July 9 saw the massacre of the British troops attacking Ft. Duquesne in Braddock's Defeat. Marching European fashion through the forests, Braddock and his men were ambushed by the French and Indians. The colonial militia, led by Col. Washington, was able to make its escape.

The British had better luck the following August on Lake Champlain. Although Crown Point resisted them, they were able to defeat a French force in the Battle of Lake George on September 8. At the south end of that lake they built Ft. William Henry. In response, the French under the gallant *Marquis de Montcalm* built Ft. Ticonderoga between the two lakes. The expedition to Niagara was abandoned.

All of this activity had occurred during ostensible peacetime, war not being declared until 1756. As with the other colonial wars, the action was dependent upon events in Europe. Until this time, the rivalry between the two great Catholic houses of Bourbon and Habsburg had provided many of the reasons for these wars, with Britain supporting the Habsburgs. At last, however, this unnatural state of affairs which had ensured the triumph both of the Protestant Revolt and of the Ottoman Turks came to an end with a treaty between France and Austria in May of 1756. By its terms, the daughter of the Holy Roman Empress, Maria Theresa, was betrothed to the Dauphin of France (later Louis XVI). Europe was now divided into two camps: Great Britain, Prussia, Hanover, and Hesse, versus France, the Empire, Austria, Saxony, Bavaria, Russia, and Sweden. War was declared, and the events in the colonies became an integral part of the world-wide conflict.

August of 1756 saw Montcalm take the British Forts Oswego and George; this disaster led to a suspension of all

British offensive plans. A year later, Ft. William Henry fell
to the French and their Indian allies. Montcalm promised
the garrison safe conduct from the fort, but he was unable to
control his Indian allies—who after all were not directly subject to him; before his horrified eyes they massacred the garrison and their dependents, as depicted in James Fenimore
Cooper's *The Last of the Mohicans.*

The next year was one of successive defeats for the French,
as post after post fell to the continually reinforced British.
Louisbourg fell after a two month long siege on July 26; Ft.
Frontenac was taken by the British August 27, followed by
Ft. Duquesne on November 25.

If 1758 was bad, 1759 was worse. Ticonderoga fell a
year to the day after Louisbourg. From that latter port, General *James Wolfe* sailed off to the St. Lawrence to try and
take the French colonial capital, Quebec. He was at first re-
pulsed at the Montmorency. But he conducted his troops
stealthily by night up to the plateau behind the city, the Plains
of Abraham, where battle was joined on September 13. The
French were completely defeated, and both Wolfe and
Montcalm were mortally wounded. There is today a monument on the sight to both of them, surely the only place in
the world where commanders of opposing armies are jointly
and equally commemorated. But as the British were break-
ing through the walls into the old city which had held them
off for a century and a half, an anonymous Frenchman carved
into the fireplace of an inn called the *Chien d'Or* —the Golden
Dog—the following lines:

> I am a dog that gnaws its bone;
> I sit and gnaw it all alone.
> A time will come, which is not yet,
> When I'll bite him by whom I'm bit.

Nevertheless, the city fell, and almost a year later Montreal and the rest of New France surrendered. In 1762, Louis XV gave Louisiana to Spain to save it from the British; everything France had owned east of the Mississippi save New Orleans was conceded to Britain in 1763, who in turn gave Spain Cuba (which they had captured) in return for Florida, which all the Spanish living there immediately left.

Pontiac's Rebellion

The defeat of the French left their Indian allies without guidance as to dealing with the changed political scene. While the new British King George III planned to be as much a father to the Indian nations as Louis XV had been (his proclamation in 1763 forbidding white settlement on Indian lands west of the Alleghenies was one sign of this), his intentions would take time to filter down to the frontier. In the meantime, Indians were no longer welcome at the formerly French posts in the old Northwest where they had always been honored guests before. Settlers took the French defeat as an invitation to seize bordering territories. In the face of this arose an imposing figure: *Pontiac*. Like King Philip before him, he was that rather rare figure among Indians: a first rate inter-tribal organizer. He was a chief by 1755, and commanded his tribe–the Ottawas–at Braddock's Defeat. Although in 1760 he had agreed to leave the English alone if they would respect him, he soon came to realize that what was at stake was not merely welcomes at forts but the ever encroaching settlers. Encouraged by French traders and hunters who informed him that he would have help from France, he resolved to drive the British out of the Northwest. On April 27, 1763, he held a grand council of all the tribes from the Great Lakes to the Lower Mississippi. His plan was relatively simple. Each of the tribes would take the nearest fort, and then united they would turn on the settlements. He reserved for himself Ft. Detroit.

He attempted to take the fort by surprise on May 7, but failed. Two days later he began the siege. Elsewhere, his plan worked perfectly. In short order, the only forts left in British hands were Detroit, Niagara, and Pitt (the former Ft. Duquesne). In July the siege of Ft. Pitt was broken by the British. Pontiac himself broke off the siege of Detroit after receiving news from the French commander of Ft. Chartres on the Mississippi that no French aid would be forthcoming on October 30. After this the rebellion petered out, partially helped by distribution of small-pox infected blankets by the British officer Colonel Henry Boquet. By the end of 1763, however, 200 settlers and traders had been killed, and about £100,000 worth of property plundered or destroyed.

Pontiac himself made peace in 1766; three years later he was killed by a Peoria Indian brave who had been bribed to do so by an English trader. The result was a ferocious reprisal the next year against the Peoria by the Pottowattomis who had been loyal allies of Pontiac. But by that time the policies of George III had borne fruit, and the tribes had given him their allegiance, thanks in no small part to his remarkable superintendent of Indian affairs, *Sir William Johnson.*

PRELUDE TO REVOLUTION

At last, British America had no real enemies to fear from the outside. But the strains and stresses in the relationship between the ruling classes of the various colonies and the Crown, which had always been there, more or less obviously, began ever increasingly to show. Further, because George III wished to restore Britain's monarchical constitution which had been eroded from the English Civil War to the accession of George I, there would of course be conflict.

Struggles Over Taxation

The wars in America had cost the British government millions of pounds; moreover, the continued necessity of defending the colonies required even more money. Up until now, the British taxpayer had footed the entire bill. But the Crown cast about for some equitable way to have the colonies pay a part of it. The oligarchies in each of the colonies, while they had no objection–through their control of the Assemblies–to taxing all the unrepresented poorer settlers, objected to being treated in the same way by the home government.

Problems began in March 1764, when Parliament passed the Sugar Act, which placed a tax upon sugar sent to the 13 colonies. As the text of the law said, "It is just and necessary that a revenue be raised in America." Immediately, *James Otis,* son of a wealthy lawyer in the province of Massachusetts, who had already made a name for himself agitating against enforcement of the Navigation Acts (which required the colonies to trade only with other British colonies–as all colonial empires did at the time), wrote a pamphlet which maintained that Parliament could not tax the colonies because the colonies were not represented therein (he doubtless would have resented a similar case being made by a local against the Assembly Otis himself sat in). At any rate, the wealthier Boston merchants made a compact not to use British goods.

The Stamp Act

March of 1765 saw another attempt to prevail upon the colonial leadership to pay their fair share. This was the Stamp Act, which required that only paper for legal documents, newsprint, and pamphlets which bore the stamp signifying payment of a small tax could be sold.

Reaction on the part of the colonial leadership, most of whom were bound not only by self-interest but also membership in the various lodges of Freemasons, was swift. *Patrick Henry* gave a speech on May 30 in Virginia's Statehouse at Williamsburg denying Parliament's right to tax the colonies. October 7 saw the convening of the Stamp Act Congress in New York, whereat representatives of the wealthy opponents of the Act gathered form all the colonies save Virginia, North Carolina, and Georgia. The delegates drew up petitions to the King and Parliament, again asserting their immunity from taxation; they adopted a *Declaration of Rights and Liberties* plainly declaring this. In our own day of IRS supremacy, we can well see the importance of the right to tax.

The arrival of stamp officers to begin collecting the tax led to demagogue-incited riots in various cities. In Boston, the house of the tax officer, *Andrew Oliver,* was looted and burned, as was that of Lieutenant Governor *Thomas Hutchinson;* in the latter case Hutchinson's manuscript of his magisterial history of the colony, along with his vital source materials, was destroyed. He later rewrote it from memory. The ring-leaders, many of whom were prominent and important men holding official positions, formed non-importation and non-consumption agreements which not only bound the signers not to use British goods, but to boycott or otherwise punish those who did. Thus, if a man refused to pay the tax, he broke the law; if he paid it, the thugs employed by the anti-Stamp Act folk would rough him up. Friends of the government in Boston were forced to lay low. In the end, the Stamp Tax brought in no money at all, and so was repealed in March of 1766. But it was done with a Parliamentary reiteration of their right to tax the colonies.

The next year, Parliament levied a tax upon glass, paper, paint, and tea brought into the colonies. It is important to remember at this point that the increase in price to the consumer was minimal. The problem for many of the wealthier circles, particularly in New England, was that a good piece of their income came from smuggling much cheaper goods from French, Dutch, Danish, or Spanish possessions, and selling them at a tremendous profit over the going rate established for goods imported from other British colonies. If all goods sold were taxed, they would have to be imported legally. This was the major reason why the colonial assemblies, dominated by such men, were resistant to the idea of paying any tax to the Crown. Beyond this problem, however, some few of the ideologues among these folk had already decided upon independence. New England had in any case always had an uneasy relationship with her Kings due to the Puritan problem.

Thus, in protest the New-York Assembly refused to make provision for the British troops sent to protect the harbor; Parliament suspended the Assembly's legislative power as a result.

Massachusetts was strife-torn in 1768. The Assembly there sent a circular letter to its equivalent bodies in the other colonies. The ministry in London demanded the letter, calling for joint resistance, be withdrawn. This demand refused (92 to 17) the Royal Governor, Sir Francis Bernard, dissolved it. The same sort of action occurred elsewhere.

In June, *John Hancock*, a known smuggler, had a sloop of his seized in Boston Harbor by the custom house officials. Hancock's allies provoked a riot, and the officials were forced to flee to Castle William on an island in the harbor. Sir Francis having left for England, Hutchinson, the Lieutenant Governor, was forced to deal with the crisis. The group centering around Hancock, Otis, *Samuel Adams, Paul Revere*, and other influential folk, had made the town and province ungovernable, putting everyone at the pleasure of a mob of their own devising. Hutchinson begged London for troops, which duly arrived in October. These restored order in Boston itself.

The same sort of men and their allies who sat in the colonial assemblies also sat on juries, both roles being in those days reserved for men of means. It was soon realized by the government that it was useless to bring before such men their friends on charge of treason. 1769 saw Parliament attempt to overcome this by resolving that acts of treason committed in the colonies could be tried in Great Britain. This was resented, of course. The Virginia House of Burgesses protested the action; Lord Dunmore, the Governor, dissolved it but similar resolutions were adopted in other colonies. Meanwhile, the Massachusetts Assembly refused to meet in Boston's State-house as long as there was a guard posted there; they adjourned to Cambridge.

For all this activity, however, worse had happened at other times in the history of the colonies. What changed the complexion of the struggle was the majority gained by the King's Friends in the House of Commons in 1770. George III was able at last to appoint a Prime Minister of his own choosing, and to assume personal rule. The whole struggle became involved, as we shall see, with much higher questions.

THE RELIGIOUS PROBLEM

Most political questions are, in essence, religious ones. The wars against the Spanish and French were religiously based, as was of course the persecution of English and other Catholics in the colonies. Beyond that, however, it was the gradual erosion of belief in Christianity of any sort which characterized the history of the colonies. The excesses of the Puritans, the gentle tolerance of the Southern Anglicans, the Inner Light of the Quakers—all resulted in the Deism of men like John Adams, Thomas Jefferson, and Benjamin Franklin. As Bernard Faÿ says of the latter: "The God that Benjamin thus adored from the bottom of his heart was not in the least like the Christian God. Rather, he resembled a....Deity that might have been dreamed of by a disciple of Plato" (*Franklin*, p.115). Deism rejected completely the idea of revealed religion, toward existing examples of which it might be either amusedly contemptuous, as was Franklin, or actively hateful, like Tom Paine.

In the place of the God of the Christians was put instead the idea of the Watchmaker-god, who set creation going but does not intervene in it. In a sense, it was the inverse of Puritanism, whose Predestination effectively prevented God from acting in the present–only in the Past could He manifest actively, in the sense of saving one's soul. It is the Deist God, in fact, whom the Masonic order claimed and claim to revere as the Grand Architect of the Universe; this was an idea which also appealed much to the scientists of the day. All three tendencies–Deistic, Masonic, and Scientificist come beautifully together in the person of Franklin's English friend, **Joseph Priestley.** Priestley was at once an inventor and chemist, pastor of the first Unitarian church in Great Britain, a Freemason, and a noted supporter (when at last the time came round) of the French Revolution.

Since there were few Catholics in the British Colonies, the task of upholding in an effective way the dictates of revealed and dogmatic Christianity fell to the Anglican establishment. Since there were no bishops in the colonies, this meant to the Royal Governors, and ultimately the King their master. It will be obvious that they were in no way adequate to the task; but they were all there was.

SUMMARY

To conclude, the history of the English colonies is the

story of the ultimate triumph of Puritanism–at first fanatical, and then latterly secularized or Deist. It is the record of
a long line of defeats of glorious causes, the victory of any
one of which might well have spelled a better present. Had
the French and Spanish triumphed, we might today be a
Catholic nation. Had the men of Merry Mount surprised
Plymouth, New England and so all Anglo-America might be
a happier place today. By the time we have reached in our
story, only two things stood in the way of complete triumph
for the sort of Deistic Puritanism we have described. One
was the very different nature of the Southern colonies, no
matter how much political considerations might have led
them to ally with New England for the moment; and allegiance to the King with connection to a larger empire. We
shall see the fate of the latter in the next book in this series.

See APPENDIX II on p.135 for a list of British Royal
Remains.

BIBLIOGRAPHY

Part I

Guéranger, Dom Prosper. *El sentido cristiano de la historia*. Buenos Aires: Ed. Iction, 1984.

Marx, Robert F. *In Quest of the Great White Gods*. New York: Crown Publishers, 1992.

Rao, Dr. John. *Americanism*. St. Paul: Remnant.

Verrill, A. Hyatt. *America's Ancient Civilizations*. New York: G.P. Putnam's Sons, 1953.

Part II

Arias, Bishop David. *Spanish Roots of America*. Bloomington: OSV Publishing, 1992.

E. Bolton, Herbert. *Wider Horizons of American History*. Notre Dame: University of Notre Dame Press, 1967.

Caponnetto, Antonio. *The Black Legends and Catholic Hispanic Culture*. St. Louis: Catholic Central Verein, 1991.

Eccles, W.J. *France in America*. New York: Harper & Row, 1972.

Gannon, Michael V. *The Cross in the Sand*. Gainesville: University of Florida Press, 1983.

Gautier, Leon. *Chivalry*. New York: Crescent Books, 1989.

Haring, C.H. *The Spanish Empire in America*. New York: Harcourt, Brace, and World, 1947.

Holbrook, Sabra. *The French Founders of North America and Their Heritage*. New York: Atheneum, 1976.

McWilliams, Carey. *North From Mexico*. New York: Greenwood Press, 1968.

Morison, Samuel Eliot. *The European Discovery of America: The Northern Voyages A.D. 500-1600*. New York: Oxford University Press, 1971.

Morison, Samuel Eliot. *The European Discovery of America: The Southern Voyages A.D. 1492-1616*. New York: Oxford University Press, 1974.

Powell, Philip Wayne. *Tree of Hate*. Vallecito: Ross House Books, 1985.

Sargent, Daniel. *Our Land and Our Lady*. New York: Longmans, Green and Co., 1939.

Waterbury, ed. Jean Parker. *The Oldest City*. St. Augustine: St. Augustine Historical Society, 1983.

Part III

Curry, Thomas J. *The First Freedoms: Church and State in America to the Passage of the First Amendment.* Oxford: Oxford University Press, 1986.

Faÿ, Bernard. *Franklin.* New York: Little, Brown, and Co., 1929.

Gannon, Michael V. *The Cross in the Sand.* Gainesville: University of Florida, 1983.

Sosin, J.M. *English America and the Restoration Monarchy of Charles II.* Lincoln: University of Nebraska Press, 1980.

Sosin, J.M. *English America and the Revolution of 1688.* Lincoln: University of Nebraska Press, 1982.

APPENDIX I

Spanish and French Royal Remains in North America

Herein are listed sites enshrining the patronage of Catholic Kings for their colonies.

FLORIDA
A. Royal Administration.

St. Augustine: Castillo San Marcos.

Matanzas Inlet: Ft. Matanzas National Monument.

Tallahassee: San Luis Archaeological and Historic site–remains of Spanish fort and mission.

St. Mark's: the ruins of Ft. San Marcos. British Rule.

St. Augustine: Government House; St. Francis Barracks; Plaza de la Constitucion.

Pensacola: Plaza Fernando VII; the ruins of Ft. San Carlos.

Fernadina: the ruins of Ft. San Carlos.

Near *Doctor's Inlet:* Hibernia Plantation, granted to the Fleming family in 1790 by King Charles IV.

Arredondo: a grant by King Ferdinand VII in 1817 to Don Fernando de la Maza de Arredondo and 200 Spanish families.

B. Royal Patronage of Religion and Education.

St. Augustine: St. Augustine's Catholic Cathedral; Nombre de Dios
  Mission.
Pensacola: St. Michael's Catholic Church.
Korona: the ruins of Tissimi Mission.

C. Monarchists.

Pensacola: the Creoles of Spanish and Black descent.
St. Augustine: two miles north of Castillo San Marcos, site of Ft. Moosa,
  settlement of freed blacks from the Carolinas established by Royal
  favor in 1738–in return, the new settlers promise, "to defend, to
  the last drop of their blood, the Crown of Spain and the holy Catholic
  Faith."

NEW YORK
Royal Patronage of Education and Religion.

St. Regis Indian Reservation: St. Regis Catholic Church, with the
  Caughnawaga Bell presented to the Indians by King Louis XV.

INDIANA
A. Royal Administration.

Ft. Wayne: the site of Ft. Miami.
Near *Lafayette:* Site of Ft. Ouiatenon.

B. Royal Patronage of Religion and Education.

Vincennes: the Catholic Cathedral of St. Francis Xavier.

C. Monarchists.

Vincennes: the Creoles, descendants of French settlers planted there
  by Royal order in 1727.

ILLINOIS
A. Royal Administration.

French Rule. *Metropolis:* Ft. Massac State Historic Park.
Near *Prairie du Rocher:* Ft. Chartres State Park and Ft. Kaskaskia
State Park.
Near *Peoria:* Ft. Creve Coeur State Park.

B. Royal Patronage of Religion and Education.

Cahokia: the Old Catholic Church of the Holy Family.
Kaskaskia: Immaculate Conception Catholic Church, with bell given
by Louis XV in 1741.

C. Monarchists.

Renault: Francophone Blacks, descendants of 500 slaves brought from
Saint Domingue in 1719, under a grant from John Law's Royal-
Chartered Mississippi Company.
Prairie du Rocher: descendants of John Law's French settlers.

WISCONSIN
A. Royal Administration.

Green Bay: site of Ft. La Baye, founded in 17th century by Commandant Nicholas Perrot for Louis XIV.
Prairie du Chien: site of Ft. St. Nicholas, established by Commandant Nicolas Perrot in 1685.

B. Royal Patronage of Religion and Education.

De Pere: Site of Saint François Xavier Mission, given by Perrot, French
Commandant at Green Bay, a silver ostensorium (now in Green Bay
Museum).

MICHIGAN
A. Royal Administration.
Detroit: founded by the French in 1701.

B. Royal Patronage of Religion and Education.
Detroit: Ste. Anne's Catholic Church, founded under royal patronage in 1705.

Mackinac Island City: Old St. Ann's Catholic Church, carried over the ice from Mackinaw City when fort transferred from mainland.

MISSISSIPPI
A. Royal Administration.
Biloxi: founded in 1721 as French centre for Mississippi Gulf coast.

Natchez: site of Ft. Rosalie, successively centre for French, British, and Spanish rule; The Elms, built by Spanish Governor Don Pedro Piernas in 1785; Hope Farm, home of Don Carlos de Grandpre, Spanish Governor 1790-1794; Airlie House, home of Don Estevan Minor, Spanish Governor 1798; Cottage Garden, house built in 1793 by Don Jose Vidal, Acting Governor of Natchez at the time of American occupation in 1798; Oakland, built by nephew of Don Estevan, has many relics of old Spanish Governor's residence, Concord.

Pascagoula: old Spanish Fort built in 1718. *Ocean Springs:* site of Ft. Maurepas, first capital (1699) of French Louisiana.

B. Royal Patronage of Religion and Education.
Natchez: Parish House of the Catholic Church of San Salvador, built by order of King Charles III of Spain in 1786 to house four Irish priests for English-speaking Catholics.

C. Monarchists.
Delisle: settled by Acadians.

ALABAMA
Royal Administration.

Mobile: Ft. Conde, seat of French, Spanish, and British Governors, and the Casket Women.

On *Dauphin Island:* site of French Governor Cadillac's court.

TENNESEE
Royal Administration.

Memphis: site of the Old Forts, the French Ft. Assumption, and the Spanish Ft. San Fernando de las Barrancas, commanded by the Dutchman, Benjamin Foy.

LOUISIANA
A. Royal Administration.

French Rule. *Nachitoches:* Ft. St. Jean Baptiste State Historic Site. Spanish Rule.

New Orleans: the Cabildo, site of Spanish administration; Charity Hospital, founded in 1736 but re-endowed by Royal Governor in 1782.

Pineville: the Rapides Cemetery with the grave of Enemund Meullion (1737-1820), commander of the Spanish Fort of Rapides.

Baton Rouge: the Pentagon, on the site of successive French, Spanish, and British forts.

Monroe: the site of Ft. Miro.

New Iberia: Shadows on the Teche Plantation, on land granted to the Weeks family by Royal Governor Carondelet in 1792.

Laurel Hill: Laurel Hill Plantation, granted to the Argue family by Charles IV.

Near *St. Francisville:* Rosale Plantation, granted to Alexander Stirling by Charles IV; Greenwood Plantation, granted to Dr. Samuel Fowler in 1788 by King Charles III.

Bains: Clover Hill Plantation, granted by King Charles IV in 1798 to Don Bernardo McDermott; Greenwood Plantation, granted by King Charles III to Dr. Samuel Flower in 1778.

Near *Big Bayou Sara:* Rosebank Plantation, granted by King Charles

IV in 1790 to Don Juan O'Connor, Alcalde (Magistrate) of West Florida under Spanish rule.

Across the Mississippi River from Ft. Jackson: Ft. St. Philip, built by Governor Carondolet on orders from King Charles IV in 1795.

Near *Thibodaux:* Rienzi Plantation, built in 1796 at request of Queen Maria Luisa of Spain, as a possible refuge in the event of Spanish defeat by the French Revolutionaries.

Near *Robeline:* Los Adais State Historic Park, site of the Presidio de Nuestra Señora del Pilar de los Adais, founded in 1721 and serving as capital of the Spanish Province of Texas until 1773.

B. Royal Patronage of Religion and Education.

New Orleans: St. Louis Catholic Cathedral; Immaculate Conception Catholic Church, with statue of the Virgin originally in private chapel of Queen Marie Amelie, consort of King Louis Phillipe; Ursuline College, founded in 1727 under the auspices of King Louis XV.

Opelousas: St. Landry Catholic Church.

St. Martinville: St. Martin de Tours Catholic Church, with a baptismal font given by King Louis XVI.

St. Gabriel: St. Gabriel Catholic Church, built on land grant made by King Charles III in 1773 to "the Parish Church of Manchac."

Labarre: St. Francis Catholic Church, with altar, pews, confessional, candlesticks, and bell (bearing date 1719), all given by King Louis XV.

St. Bernard: St. Bernard's Catholic Church, built on land granted the Parish by Spanish Viceroy Bernardo Galvez in 1778.

C. Monarchists.

Nachitoches: the Chamard House–built in 1735 by Bourbon descendant Andre Chamard, who was later knighted by Louis XVI. The Acadians, who began to arrive after their expulsion from Nova Scotia in 1755.

In *St. Bernard Parish:* the Isleños, descendants of Canary Islanders sent to Louisiana by King Charles III of Spain in 1778 and 1779.

New Iberia: descendants of Canary Islanders sent to the spot by King Charles III of Spain in 1788.

ARKANSAS
Royal Administration.

At *Arkansas Post:* site of seat of French and Spanish Governors.

MISSOURI
A. Royal Administration.

Ste. Genevieve: François Vallé House, home of François Vallé, Spanish Commandant of Ste. Genevieve District from 1783 to 1804.

Florissant: Casa Alvarez, home of Augustine Alvarez, Deputy Commandant of the Spanish District of San Fernando de Florissant in the 1790's.

Portage des Sioux: the Common Field, granted to the village by the King of Spain.

Matson: the Daniel Boone Farm, granted to the great frontiersman by King Charles IV in 1799.

B. Royal Patronage of Education and Religion.

Fredericktown: St. Michael Catholic Church, in the rectory of which is a painting given by a king of Spain, *The Holy Family.*

C. Monarchists.

Cape Girardeau: home and grave of Don Luis Lorimier, half-breed Shawnee chief, supporter of the British during the Revolution, afterwards commandant for the Spanish of the District of Cape Girardeau.

IOWA
Royal Administration.

Spanish Rule. *Dubuque:* grave of Julien Dubuque, to whom the city (then called *Les Mines d'Espagne*) was granted by King Charles III in 1788.

Montrose: site of 1799 grant by King Charles IV to French Canadian Louis Honore Tesson, with instructions to "plant trees, sow seeds,

teach the science of agriculture to the Indians, and spread the te-
nets of the Catholic Faith."

TEXAS
A. Royal Administration.

Spanish rule. *San Antonio:* the Spanish Governors' Palace, with the
Habsburg double-eagle on the keystone over the entrance and the
date 1749.
Menard: Presidio San Luis de las Amarillas, founded in 1757.
Presidio: site of Presidio del Norte.
Nacogdoches: reproduction of the Old Stone Fort, erected originally in
1779.
Goliad: the Presidio Nuestra Señora de Loreto de la Bahia, founded in
1749.

B. Royal Patronage of Religion and Education.

San Antonio: San Fernando Catholic Cathedral, built at royal expense
in 1738, with several *objects d'art* given by Phillip V of Spain; Mission Concepcion founded in 1731; Mission San Jose, with three
paintings in chapel given by Phillip V; Mission San Francisco de la
Espada founded in 1731; Mission San Juan Capistrano, founded
also in 1731. El Paso, the missions of Corpus Christi de la Ysleta del
Sur, San Elizario, and La Purisima Concepcion del Socorro.
Laredo: San Augustin Catholic Church, founded at royal expense in
1767.
Weches: Mission San Francisco de los Tejas, originally built in 1690–
now a reproduction.
Refugio: site of Mission Nuestra Señora del Refugio.
Menard: Mission Santa Cruz or San Saba.
Goliad: Mission Nuestra Señora del Espiritu Santo de Zuñiga, built in
1749.

C. Monarchists.

San Antonio: site of the Battle of the Medina, where, on 18 August
1813, the Spanish General Joaquin Arredondo with an army of
Royalists annihilated a band of Mexican Revolutionaries and Americans who had occupied San Antonio.

Nacogdoches: site of repulse of American filibusterers in 1819 by towns-people loyal to the King of Spain.

NEW MEXICO
A. Royal Administration.

Santa Fe: called the Royal City of the Holy Faith of St. Francis; the Palace of the Governors, built in 1609, and seat of Royal adminis-tration from that year until (with the exception of the 1680-1692 Pueblo Revolt) Mexican independence in 1821–and of the Imperial Mexican rule for the year after that.

Albuquerque: Old Town Plaza, granted to the City by King Phillip V of Spain in 1706.

Peña Blanca: a Spanish village set between two Indian Pueblos, whose legal problem with these neighbors on two occasions had to be sent to Spain for judgment by the king. The eighteen Indian Pueblos in the state all enjoy royal land grants, and their civil heads are gover-nors whose canes are symbolic of royal authority.

Los Lunas: granted to the Candelaria family in 1716, passing into the hands of the Luna family, whose grant was confirmed by the US in 1899 (one of the few New Mexican families to receive such confir-mation).

Socorro: granted to 21 families (whose descendants still live there) by King Ferdinand VII in 1817.

Santa Cruz: the second royal city in New Mexico, founded in 1692 as "The Royal City of the Holy Cross of the Spanish Mexicans of the King Our Master Charles II."

La Ventana: Ojo Del Espiritu Santo, land grant given by the Spanish King to the De Baca family, and retained by them until 1934.

B. Royal Patronage of Religion and Education.

Santa Fe: San Miguel Catholic Church, built and restored by the royal governors in 1636, 1693, and 1710.

Albuquerque: San Felipe de Neri Catholic Church, financed by King Philip V in 1706.

San Miguel del Bado: San Miguel del Bado Catholic Church, built in 1806 with royal patronage.

Pecos National Park: with ruins of Mission Church of Nuestra de Los Angeles, built at behest of King Philip III. The eighteen Indian

Pueblos all boast churches built at royal expense, as do the older
Hispano villages.

Acoma Pueblo: San Esteban Rey Catholic Church, has a picture of St.
Joseph given to the church by King Philip IV in 1629.

Santa Cruz: Holy Cross Catholic Church, with a 1797 letter from
Charles IV of Spain concerning the Indians.

C. Monarchists.

Belen: founded for *Genizaros*, Indian captives rescued by the Spanish
from Apaches and Comanches, by the royal authorities.

Abiquiu: another *Genizaro* settlement, in this case, Tlaxcalans, whose
prince was an ally of the King of Spain.

ARIZONA
A. Royal Administration.

A part of Spanish province of New Mexico.

Tucson: Presidio Park.

Tubac: Presidio ruins.

B. Royal Patronage of Religion and Education.

Near *Tucson:* Missions San Xavier del Bac and Tumacacori.

CALIFORNIA
A. Royal Administration.

Monterey: the Old Customhouse; the Presidio.

San Diego: Presidio Park.

San Francisco: the Presidio's Officers' Club (originally the Spanish
Commandante's headquarters).

Santa Barbara: the reconstructed Presidio.

Sonoma: the Presidio.

Los Angeles: the Plaza, where royal decree ordered settlement.

El Camino Real (the King's Highway): linking presidios and missions.

B. Royal Patronage of Religion and Education.

All of the missions were royally decreed, and endowed with gifts.

Monterey: the Royal Presidio Chapel.

San Francisco: Mission Dolores, with picturing showing St. Joseph being reverenced by Pope Pius VI and King Charles IV, given by the latter.

Santa Barbara: Mission Santa Barbara. Santa Cruz, Mission Santa Cruz. Carmel, Mission San Carlos Borromeo.

Lompoc: Mission La Purisima Concepcion.

Sonoma: Mission San Francisco Solano.

San Rafael: Mission San Rafael.

Santa Clara: Mission Santa Clara.

San Juan Bautista: Mission San Juan Bautista.

San Miguel: Mission San Miguel.

San Luis Obispo: Mission San Luis Obispo.

Solvang: Mission Santa Ynez.

Ventura: Mission San Buenaventura, with painting of St. Bonaventure given by Charles III.

San Juan Capistrano: Mission San Juan Capistrano.

Oceanside: Mission San Luis Rey.

San Fernando: Mission San Fernando.

San Diego: Mission San Diego.

Fremont: Mission San Jose.

San Gabriel: Mission San Gabriel, which has both a font and crown-topped Blessed Sacrament lamp, alike gifts of King Charles III of Spain.

ONTARIO
Royal Administration.

Midland: Ste. Marie-among-the-Hurons, reconstruction of French fort and mission with Huron Indian village near shrine of the Canadian Martyrs.

Kingston: site of Ft. Frontenac.

QUEBEC
A. Royal Administration.

Montréal: Château de Ramezay, built in 1705 by the French Governor of Montréal, Claude de Ramezay, and now housing a museum.

Trois Rivières: the Old Recollet Monastery, founded 1698 and later residence of French Governor; Godefroy de Tonnancourt Manor,

granted by Louis XIV to de Seigneuret in 1700; Manoire Boucher
de Niverville, granted to de Chastelain by Louis XV in 1740.

Quebec: Chateau Frontenac Hotel, on the site of Chateau St. Louis,
residence of Governors of New France.

Chambly: Ft. Chambly National Park, massive fortification built by
French between 1709 and 1711.

B. Royal Patronage of Religion and Education.

Montréal: Notre Dame Catholic Church, originally founded in 1656,
with silver statue of the Madonna presented by Louis XV; Seminary
of St. Sulpice built in 1710 as headquarters of Sulpician order,
granted seigneurie of Montréal by Louis XIV in 1663.

NOVA SCOTIA
Royal Administration.

Aulac: Ft. Beausejour National Park, built 1751-1755 at order of
French Governor de la Jonquière.

Annapolis Royal: Ft. Anne National Historic Park, built originally by
the French in 1702.

Louisbourg: rebuilt city-fortress begun under Louis XV in 1717.

APPENDIX II

British Royal Remains

Here are a list of places where the student may see surviving evidence of the British Crown's concern for its American subjects.

MASSACHUSETTS.
A. Royal Administration.

Boston: the Old State House with its Royal Coat of Arms on the exterior, and State [King] street; the Ancient and Honorable Artillery Company, founded in 1638 as daughter unit of Honorable Artillery Company of London.

Williamsburg: the Silas Snow Farm, granted to Samuel Barber by King George II, in a deed still extant. Cape Cod, where the revival of the name "King's Highway" caused trouble so late as 1937.

Mashpee: The resident Indian tribe appealed to King George III for self-government, received it, supported the rebels and were rewarded after the Revolution by losing their autonomy again until 1834.

B. Royal Patronage of education and religion.

Boston: King's Chapel, with its intact Royal Governor's pew with canopy; Old North (Christ Episcopal) Church, built in 1723 with its bells inscribed "We are the first ring of bells cast for the British

Empire in North America."

Newbury: St. Paul's Episcopal church, originally Queen Anne's Chapel, built in 1711.

MAINE
Royal administration.

Phipps Point: site of childhood home of Sir William Phipps, Maine native who rose to become Royal Governor of Massachusetts during Salem trials. In Bath, Peterson House, home of the King's timber agent.

Wicasset: the Pownalborough Courthouse.

Castine: Ft. George, built by British during Revolution.

Portland: the site of Ft. New Casco.

NEW HAMPSHIRE
A. Royal Administration.

Portsmouth: The Wentworth Home, residence of John Wentworth, last Royal Governor, from which he was driven by a mob; Old State House, former seat of Provincial Assembly.

Odiorne's Point: Benning Wentworth Mansion, palatial residence of penultimate Royal Governor.

New Castle: Library maintains copy of town charter granted by William and Mary in 1693; Ft. Constitution, originally Ft. William and Mary, seized by the rebels in 1774.

Randolph: granted by King George III in 1772 to John Durnand and others of London.

B. Royal Patronage to Religion and Education.

Portsmouth: St. John's Episcopal Church (formerly Queen's Chapel) with pulpit, two mahogany chairs, and communion set (all bearing the Royal Arms) presented by Queen Caroline.

Hanover: Dartmouth University, established under a charter granted by George III in 1769; at the University, gifts from Royal Governor John Wentworth, including a silver punchbowl still used at college functions, a large and ornate badge presented to each president at his inauguration, and a large tract of land in the north of the colony still called the Dartmouth College Grant.

Nashua: The Public Library maintains original charter from George II to the Town of Dunstable given in 1746.

RHODE ISLAND
A. Royal Administration

Rhode Island a Corporate Colony with elected Governor.

Providence: Old State House, one of two centers of government under the Crown; 1663 Charter granted by King Charles II on display outside Senate Chambers in State House, site of Jabez Bowens House, from the balcony of which the accession of George III was proclaimed.

Newport: Old Colony House, one of two centers of government under the Crown; Newport Artillery Armory, headquarters of the Newport Artillery Company, chartered in 1741; the Wanton-Lyman-Hazard House, in which Governor Joseph Wanton lived when he was deposed in 1775–he also owned the Hunter House; Dudley Place, home of Charles Dudley, Royal Collector of Customs for Rhode Island, and forced to flee to England in 1775.

Portsmouth: Honyman House, home of James Honyman, Jr., King's Advocate for the Court of Vice-Admiralty, and confiscated after British withdrawal in 1779.

B. Royal Patronage of Religion and Education.

Providence: St. John's Episcopal Church, called until 1822 Queen's Chapel.

Newport: Trinity Episcopal Church, with a bell and communion service donated by Queen Anne in 1709, a crown on the spire forgotten for removal by the rebels, and an organ surmounted by a crown on one side and a miter on the other; the Redwood Library and Athenaeum, organized in 1730 and incorporated in 1747, it received a gift of 84 books from George II.

CONNECTICUT
Royal Administration.

Hartford: the barracks of the Governor's Foot Guards, and their 18th century British uniforms.

Madison: the Stevens Farm, operated by the same family since 1675, whose current representatives still hold the original grant to the property given them by Charles II.

Southbury: a Common called the "King's Land," because, although property of the Crown, it was not seized by the town at the Revolution, and so to this day is held to belong still to the Sovereign.

NEW YORK
A. Royal Administration.

New York City: civic coat-of-arms identical to-day to the one granted by the King, save for the replacement of the crown by an eagle; Grant of Pelham Manor to Thomas Pell (ancestor of Senator Claiborne Pell) confirmed by James II; Federal Hall (on site of Government House); Bowling Green, site of famous equestrian statue of George III pulled down and melted (although pieces of it are in the New York Historical Society collection), while ornamental crowns on fence pickets were snapped off; The Customs House, site of Ft. Amsterdam (later Ft. George) which contained Governor's House built for Peter Stuyvesant and used by all Dutch and English Governors thereafter until 1783); the New York Chamber of Commerce, chartered by George III in 1770; New York Hospital, chartered by George III in 1771.

Crown Point: ruins of Ft. St. Frederic , built by the French; Ft. Crown Point, built to replace the latter by the British.

Ticonderoga: Ft. Ticonderoga, built by French–major British garrison until seized by rebels under Ethan Allen.

Harmon: Van Cortlandt Manor House, built in 1749 and boasting in front room charter from William III to Oloff Van Cortlandt, first Lord of the Manor.

Oswego: Ft. Ontario, built by the British in 1756 and occupied by them until 1796.

Youngstown: Ft. Niagara, built by the French in 1725, occupied by the British and relinquished by them in 1796.

Beacon-Newburgh Ferry: operating under charter granted in 1743 by King George II to Alexander Colden.

Hyde Park: St. James's Episcopal Church, built 1811 on land donated by Dr. Samuel Bard from the tract granted his family by Queen Anne.

Wappingers' Falls: the Treasure Chest Tavern, in which is original charter granted by George II for the site.

B. Royal Patronage of Religion and Education.

New York City: St. Paul's Episcopal Chapel with Royal Governor's pew; Trinity Episcopal Church, still legally owned by H.M. the Queen; the Queen's Farm, the land west of Broadway to the Hudson bounded by Christopher and Fulton Streets–given by Queen Anne to Trinity, it remains a large part of that Church's endowment; St. Paul's Episcopal Chapel, with Royal Governor's pew; King's College (now Columbia University) founded in 1754 under charter of George II New York Society Library, although founded in 1754, chartered by George III in 1772.

The Bronx: Fordham Dutch Reformed Church, organized in 1696 under charter granted by William III.

Staten Island: St. Andrew Episcopal Church, chartered by Queen Anne in 1713 and presented by her with communion silver and a bell; Old Dutch Reformed Church, erected on land donated by Royal Governor Hunter in 1714.

Albany: St. Peter's Episcopal Church, with replica of communion service presented by Queen Anne in 1712.

Fort Hunter: Queen Anne's Episcopal Parsonage, built in 1712 at the Queen's order as part of the Royal Chapel of the Mohawks, transferred after the Revolution (with the communion silver) to Brantford, Ontario.

Clyde: St. John's Episcopal Church, with organ originally presented by Queen Anne to New York's Trinity Church.

NEW JERSEY
A. Royal Administration.

Burlington: West Jersey Proprietors' Office, headquarters of the successor of the original grantees of West Jersey, still functioning under the charter granted them by Charles II; Governor Franklin Estate, site of the home of Governor William Franklin, last Royal Governor of New Jersey, son of Benjamin, who suffered imprisonment in this house and exile for his loyalty.

Perth Amboy: The Westminster, residence of Governor William Franklin, where he was imprisoned for a time in punishment for attempting to convene the colonial assembly; East Jersey Proprietors' Office, equivalent of their colleagues in Burlington.

Salem: Bradway House, residence of several Royal Governors.

B. Royal Patronage of Religion and Education.

Burlington: Library, functioning under 1757 charter from King George II, and boasts a painting of him; Old St. Mary's Episcopal Church, with communion plate given by Queen Anne.

New Brunswick: Rutgers University, founded as Queen's College in 1766 with charter granted by George III. Monmouth Battlefield, Old Tennent Presbyterian church, chartered by George II in 1749.

Shrewsbury: Christ Episcopal Church, displaying in its entry way the charter from George II, and carved canopies over the Royal Governor's pew.

PENNSYLVANIA
A. Royal Administration.

Philadelphia: Independence Hall, originally State House of the Province; Bartram's Gardens, botanical gardens founded by John Bartram, "American Botanist to King George III."

Pittsburgh: the Fort Pitt Blockhouse, part of fort erected by British employed Swiss Colonel Henry Bouquet to replace the French Ft. Duquesne built nearby.

Reading: Penn's Commons, city park reserved as public common for the town in 1748 by the Penn family, Lords Proprietor under the Crown of the Province of Pennsylvania.

Pennsbury: Pennsbury Manor, estate of William Penn, to whom King James II granted Pennsylvania.

Waterford: ruins of Ft. Le Boeuf, built by the French in 1753, and occupied by the British six years later.

B. Royal Patronage of Religion and Education.

Philadelphia: Christ Episcopal Church, a medallion of George II in the front façade, over the large palladian window, as well as several Royal Coats of Arms in the church, and a silver communion set given by Queen Anne in 1708.

DELAWARE
A. Royal Administration.

New Castle: the former State House (now County Courthouse); the Green where the State House pictures of the King and Queen were burned on 4 July 1776.

B. Royal Patronage of Religion and Education.

New Castle: Immanuel Episcopal church, recipient of altar cloths, pulpit, a box of glass, and communion silver from Queen Anne, only the latter of which remain.

Middletown: Old St. Anne's Episcopal church, with a piece of an altar cloth embroidered with the silk letters A.R. (*Anne Regina*), given by Queen Anne.

Broad Creek Hundred: Christ Episcopal church, formerly possessing a Bible given in 1777 by George III's Queen, Charlotte.

MARYLAND AND THE DISTRICT OF COLUMBIA
A. Royal Administration.

Annapolis: the State House, built in 1772 as home of colonial legislature–still used by State legislature; the Old Treasury, built in 1695 and used as Governor's Council Chamber; McDowell Hall–St. John's College's administration building, built as Royal Governor's mansion in 1742; the Nicholson House, home of Royal Governor and meeting place of Assembly 1694-1709.

Near *Annapolis*: Whitehall, summer seat 1766 to 1769 of Royal Governor Horatio Sharpe. In Elkridge, site of port of entry outfitted with special British excise and customs agents for assessing tobacco shipped from thence.

St. Mary's City: St. Mary's Statehouse, reconstruction of first Maryland seat of government first erected in 1676.

B. Royal Patronage of Religion and Education.

Annapolis: St. Anne's Episcopal Church, with communion silver presented by King William III in 1695; St. John's College, established as successor to King William's School, established under Royal Charter in 1696.

Kingsville: St. John's Episcopal Church, with communion set presented by Queen Anne.

Church Hill: St. Luke's Episcopal Church, chancel-tablets of the Lord's Prayer and the Ten Commandments, both presented by Queen Anne.

Centerville: St. Paul's Episcopal church, with chalice and flagon given by Queen Anne.

Church Creek: Old Trinity Episcopal Church, possessing a chalice given by Queen Anne and a red velvet cushion upon which she knelt at her coronation.

Snow Hill: All Hallows Episcopal Church, with a Bible dated 1701, and presented by Queen Anne.

VIRGINIA

A. Royal Administration.

Williamsburg: the Governor's Palace, home of the Royal Governors; the Colonial Capitol, seat of the House of Burgesses and the Council. Norfolk, granted a charter by George II in 1736, received also a civic mace in 1753, still kept there.

Walkerton: against whom in 1748 the House of Burgesses passed a bill to prevent their inhabitants thereat from building wooden chimneys or raising hogs—George II vetoed this in 1753; Enfield, granted to the Waller family by Charles II.

Pamunkey Indian Reservation: which tribe, by the 1677 treaty securing its land, acknowledges "their immediate dependency on" the King of England, in token of which the tribe was given a velvet and silver "crown."

B. Royal Patronage of Religion and Education.

Williamsburg: Bruton Parish Episcopal Church, the place of worship of the Royal Governors, complete with canopied pew for them bearing the Royal Arms, and three communion sets presented by three different Governors; the College of William and Mary chartered by those monarchs in 1693 under the name "Their Majesties' Royal College of William and Mary, in Virginia," and granted a coat of arms by the College of Arms in London the following year.

Aquia: site of the Brenton Tract, granted by James II in 1686 for the free exercise of the Catholic religion.

Pungoteague: St. George's Episcopal Church, with communion service given by Queen Anne.

Eastville: Hungar's Episcopal Church, with vestments presented by Queen Anne.

Port Royal: Vauter's Episcopal Church with communion service presented by Queen Anne.

WEST VIRGINIA
Royal Administration.

Ona: center of Savage Grant, given by George III to John Savage.

NORTH CAROLINA
A. Royal Administration.

New Bern: Tryon's Palace, completely restored seat of government for the colony, and model for Government House at Nassau in the Bahamas.

Fayetteville: the Purdy House, on land granted to the Purdy family before the Revolution by George III.

Aberdeen: Old Bethesda Presbyterian Church, built on five-acre tract granted to John Patterson by King George III. Mount Holly, built on a grant from George II.

B. Royal Patronage of Religion and Education.

New Bern: Christ Episcopal Church, with communion service, Bible, and prayer-book given by George II in 1752.

Edenton: St. Paul's Episcopal Church, with silver chalice given in 1701 by Francis Nicholson, Royal Governor of North Carolina.

Brunswick: ruins of St. Philip's Episcopal Church, formerly His Majesty's Chapel in the Colony, where the Royal Governors worshipped.

Bath: St. Thomas Episcopal Church, with silver altar candelabra given by George II, and a bell and (formerly) a chalice given by Queen Anne.

SOUTH CAROLINA
A. Royal Administration.

Charleston: the Huger House, residence of Lord William Campbell, last Royal Governor of the Province who was forced to flee in 1775; the William Bull House, residence of William Bull, Jr., Lieutenant Governor to Lord William Campbell; the Stuart House, residence of Colonel John Stuart, Commissioner of Indian Affairs in the South, who was forced to flee for his loyalty in 1775; the County Court house, built within the walls of the former Government House after it burned in 1788.

Columbia: the State Capitol, housing in the Senate Chamber the Sword of State, and in the House of Representatives, the mace (bearing the Royal Arms of Great Britain, the arms of Hanover, and those of the Province of South Carolina), used by their pre-revolutionary predecessors, the Council and House of Commons.

Georgetown: the Winyah Indigo Society Hall, seat of a fraternal organization given a charter by George II in 1758.

Kingstree: settled in 1732 around a white pine earlier marked to reserve it as a potential mast for His Majesty's ships—after that, all the white pines in the area were so reserved in land grants, and to this day the streets of Kingstree curve around so as to preserve them.

Society Hill: center of Welsh Neck, a tract granted by George II in 1736.

Roebuck: Fredonia, ancestral home of the Moore family, granted to them by George III in 1763.

Union: Forest Hills Estate, granted to Thomas Flectall by George III in 1772.

B. Royal Patronage of Religion and Education.

Goose Creek: Goose Creek Church, still bears the Royal Arms over the chancel.

GEORGIA
Royal Administration.

Savannah: Wright Square named after last Royal Governor, James Wright (forced to flee in January 1776, returned with British troops to run colony in 1779, staying until final withdrawal); Telfair House, mansion built on site of Government House fled by Governor Wright.

Outside *Savannah*: Lebanon, a plantation granted by King George II in 1756 and 1758 to James Devaux and Philip Delegal; Wild Hern Plantation, granted by George II in 1755 to Francis Harris.

On *St. Simon's Island*: the ruins of Ft. Frederica; Refuge Plantation, granted by King George III in 1765 to James Houstoun McIntosh. Near *Darien*, Ft. King George State Historic Site.

Waynesboro: Bellevue Plantation, granted by King George III in 1767 to Samuel Eastlake, a copy of which grant, signed by Royal Governor James Wright remains in the family's possession.

QUEBEC
Royal Patronage of Religion and Education.

Quebec: Anglican Cathedral of the Holy Trinity, with communion silver given by George III in 1768.

NOVA SCOTIA
Royal Patronage of Religion and Education.

Lunenburg: St. John's Anglican Church, founded by royal charter in 1754, with communion vessels given by George III, and a choir entitled to wear red cassocks as royal foundation.